WEAVING THE SERMON

1989

WEAVING
THE SERMON

*Preaching in a Feminist
Perspective*

CHRISTINE M. SMITH

1989

Westminster/John Knox Press
Louisville, Kentucky

For permission to reprint, grateful acknowledgment is made to the following:
BEACON PRESS, for excerpts from *Making the Connections* by Beverly Wildung Harrison and Carol S. Robb, copyright © 1985 by Beverly Wildung Harrison and Carol S. Robb, and from *Sexism and God-Talk* by Rosemary Radford Ruether, copyright © 1983 by Rosemary Radford Ruether; SUSAN RAY BEEHLER and (for the last verse) LINDA COVELESKIE, for "Steppin' Out"; BETH BRANT, for "Rug of Woven Magic" from *A Gathering of Spirit,* Beth Brant, ed., Sinister Wisdom Books, 1984; BRETHREN PRESS, for Julia Esquivel, "Indian Tapestry," from *Threatened with Resurrection: Prayers and Poems from an Exiled Guatemalan,* © 1982; HARCOURT BRACE JOVANOVICH, INC., for Alice Walker, "We Alone," from *Horses Make a Landscape Look More Beautiful,* copyright © 1984 by Alice Walker; HEREFORD MUSIC, for Holly Near, "The Great Peace March," and Judy Small, "Speaking Hands and Hearing Eyes"; LITTLE, BROWN AND COMPANY, for an excerpt from *Annie and the Old One* by Miska Miles, text copyright © 1971 by Miska Miles; JAN POWERS MILLER, for "Makin' Room for the Silences"; W. W. NORTON & COMPANY, INC. for "Who Said It Was Simple?" from *Chosen Poems, Old and New* by Audre Lorde, copyright © 1982, 1976, 1974, 1973, 1970, 1968 by Audre Lorde.

Book design by Gene Harris

First edition

Published by Westminster/John Knox Press
Louisville, Kentucky

PRINTED IN THE UNITED STATES OF AMERICA

9 8 7 6 5 4 3

Library of Congress Cataloging-in-Publication Data

Smith, Christine M.
  Weaving the sermon.

  Includes index.
  1. Preaching. 2. Feminism—Religious aspects—
Christianity. 3. Women clergy. I. Title.
BV4235.F44S63 1989   251'.0088042   88-27942
ISBN 0-664-25031-9 (pbk.)

For my family—
Betty, Raymond,
Pam, Charles,
Elizabeth, Bev, Ida

Contents

Acknowledgments

As I contemplate the many people who share in this creation, I am reminded again of the interwoven quality of life. The gifts of countless people form the web of support, the tapestry of beauty and truth, and the cloth of woven vision that has sustained, deepened, and transformed this book.

The feminist women within the Christian church, with their critical powers, vision, and living witness, are the women to whom I am most indebted. These lay and clergy women who are committed to the transformation of an institution, and to new definitions and expressions of ministry as we have known them, shape the heart and soul of my work. I can only hope that this contribution about preaching from a feminist perspective will further the radical change we all so passionately desire and work toward.

Four colleagues have supported this work from its inception, and I am grateful for their collegiality and friendship: Doug Adams, Clare Fischer, Edwina Hunter, and Carter Heyward. Their faithful strands of wisdom, scholarly insight, creativity, and collaboration have been paramount in this project.

Letty Russell has been a steadfast believer in the vision of this book. She raised her voice on behalf of my work, so that my voice could speak. She is an incredibly faithful woman, who knows how to be an advocate for other women with a spirit of mutuality and empowerment. Cynthia Thompson, editor at Westminster Press, gave me added confidence in the quality of my words and thoughts and encouraged me to stay true to my own integrity. Joe Herman typed the final copy of the manuscript. His efficiency and patience have been gifts beyond belief.

Sandra Boyd, Gina Book, Christie Neuger, and Judith Sanderson have been sources of laughter, rest and renewal, tenderness, and peace. I feel great thanksgiving for the group we share.

Tom Long, my primary colleague at Princeton Theological Seminary and my friend, continues to inspire me with his own preaching ministry. The power and creativity he weaves into his spoken proclamations always leave me laughing . . . weeping . . . changed. The students at the seminary provide motivation, graciously receive my thoughts, and critique and deepen them.

To reserve these final lines for those most personally woven into my life seems only appropriate. In the past year five friends have loved and cared for me in the daily moments of every day. They have become a central part of the loom of my life and have woven hope into my being at every turn. Elizabeth Vandegrift, Jennifer Manlowe, Kathy Greider, Jane Heckels, and Barbara Weaver—thank you. Then, too, Bev Shaw has been central to the wholeness of my life for almost fifteen years, providing a foundation of love. And Ida Thornton continues to be a primary source of grace and inspiration. Finally, there are simply no words to express the sacred love my parents, Betty and Raymond Smith, have poured into me. The essence of who they are, along with my sister, Pam Smith, is embodied in the strands of my entire being and all my commitments to faithful living. They are the first of many who set me on my way in this world . . . to weave.

1

Weaving:
Vision and Craft

Weaving has many faces: it is a craft, a medium for working directly with fundamental materials to create joyful mixtures of textures and colors, to feel the accomplishment of mastering the tools and learning the steps. . . . It is an art, an expression of our time, which can have the brilliance of a painting, the dimension of sculpture, the shape of invention, and the form of imagination. It is functional, intimately related to us through our daily use of fabrics. It is an industrial product made speedily by the power loom, but unchanged in its basic construction of interlocking threads, and it is as individual as its creator will make it. It is a tool for the educator and a technique for the therapist; it is romantic and sober, ancient and contemporary.[1]

Within the recent literature of feminist theology, women's published sermons, feminist spirituality, and women's psychology, weaving emerges as an organizing image in women's lives. Using this image of weaving as a central lens of understanding, I will explore several strands of feminist thought and insight that are producing a new understanding of the preaching task.

The Strands of the Weaving

Several questions focus my work in the development of weaving as a metaphor for preaching from a feminist perspective. (1) *The nature of pastoral intimacy and authority in the preaching*

task: Are there distinctive ways women weave their lives with
the lives of the community in the preaching act? (2) *The prophetic nature of preaching in confronting and challenging:* How
do the contributions of Christian feminists weave a fuller understanding of Christian theology and faith into women's and
men's preaching? (3) *The nature of vision and hope in preaching:*
How do women and men weave a pluralistic and integrated
vision into their preaching, a vision informed by global feminism? (4) *The nature of style in the preaching act:* Do women
weave distinctive stylistic elements into the preaching act?

I am convinced that when the strands of women's experience,
thinking, and embodiment are interwoven they comprise a large
portion of the distinctiveness of women's preaching from a feminist perspective. I have chosen to explore such a breadth of
topics because at present we need a broad picture of the contribution of feminist women to the larger field of homiletics. This
work is an attempt to begin to name and develop some of the
key strands of transformation at work in preaching from a
feminist perspective.

Even though I will often focus my attention on how these
transforming strands of feminism are reflected in the lives and
preaching of women, the critique and vision of feminist theology, art, and literature are relevant and important considerations for all homileticians and preachers today. All preachers
who take feminist theology, psychology, and philosophy seriously will be asked throughout this book to reevaluate and
redefine their own preaching, and question many of the basic
assumptions they have made about the nature and act of proclamation. As the weaving metaphor unfolds, it asks each of us to
look again at our own preaching style, theology, hermeneutical
principles, understandings of authority, and visions of transformation.

In the homiletics literature there is little scholarship about
women's preaching. Growing numbers of women have been
preaching in mainline denominations for ten to fifteen years.
Within Roman Catholic churches as well, one finds increasing
participation by women in the preaching ministry of the parish.
Yet even in the midst of this reality there are no substantial
published works on the distinctive voice of women preachers,

and there is virtually no scholarship on feminist perspectives on preaching. While there are many books and articles today dealing with feminist theology, ethics, and biblical hermeneutics, there is an overwhelming absence of feminist scholarship in homiletics. This absence may suggest a lack of consensus regarding the distinctive quality of women's preaching and may also indicate how difficult it is to name and describe particular feminist elements of this distinctiveness.

Particularities of the Research

Let me state from the onset a basic working assumption, which becomes the shaping parameter of my research. I *do* assume that there is some qualitative distinctiveness surrounding the preaching of feminist women. Many scholars in the field of homiletics and many preachers do not affirm this assumption. I do not assert this as a value judgment, but rather as a personal, theological, and pastoral conviction. I believe it is this distinctiveness, however subtle and difficult to articulate fully, that will finally reveal to us a new perspective for preaching.

The assertion that there is a distinctive quality that many women bring to the preaching task must be clarified. I believe that there is distinctive female experience and particularity that all women bring to the task of preaching that is different from the particularity that men bring to the act and craft of preaching. This female experience and the impact of specific gender enculturation I will address in the next chapter. This aspect of distinctiveness is important, but I am primarily interested in the preaching of women and men who would self-consciously describe their theology and work as feminist. This means that the primary focus of my research is on mainline Protestant women, primarily white, middle-class, North American preachers who, much like myself, have been influenced by feminist scholarship as it continues to permeate all major areas of theological education and every aspect of Christian ministry. The connections have not yet been explicitly made between this body of feminist theological scholarship and the discipline of homiletics. In this work, therefore, I will seek to weave threads between feminist scholarship and homiletical practice. I have chosen this clear

feminist focus because I believe it is the perspective that prom-
ises to transform preaching most radically for the contemporary
Christian church.

The content of my research has not focused on structured
interviews of women preachers, nor is it primarily concerned
with detailed analyses of women's sermons. Rather, the primary
task of this work is to show the major influence of feminist
scholarship upon the evolution of the kind of preaching best
described as preaching from a feminist perspective. My own
experience as a United Methodist clergywoman and woman
preacher for the past twelve years and the experiences of many
clergywomen I encounter serve as foundational material for
many of the assertions I will make.

Because of my focus on theological education and feminist
theology, I assume that my research describes clergywomen's
experiences more adequately than it does the experience of laywomen who preach. I am not unaware, however, that laywomen
are preachers at various levels of the church's ministry and that
much of my research may describe their experiences and commitments. Many Christian laywomen embrace the critique and
vision of feminist theology, are committed to new understandings of the preaching task, and strive to embody new styles and
methods of preaching. The contribution of laywomen preachers
in the life of the church is by no means insignificant. I focus on
the preaching of clergywomen as a means of discerning a feminist approach to preaching because this is my own primary
experience, and this is the community of women preachers with
whom I am most familiar.

I am very aware also that the scope of my work primarily
applies to the preaching of white Protestant women. I have read
Black women's sermons, studied some of their scholarly work
concerning the craft and act of preaching, and had lengthy
discussions with Black women about preaching within the Black
church experience. It is clear that many Black women experience preaching quite differently from white women. The Black
church as cultural and religious context has often had a profound influence on the lives of Black women who preach. This
experience is not mine, however, and I am aware of what limited
knowledge I hold in this area. It would be presumptuous indeed

to attempt a description of women's preaching that emerges from within cultural, ethnic, and economic situations radically different from my own. Many of the questions I raise throughout this work will be an attempt to acknowledge those limitations honestly. I will, however, attempt to raise questions of common concern for all feminist, or womanist, women who preach today. There are several issues and concerns I will raise where feminist women might begin to share their particular insights and discoveries about preaching that do emerge from within very distinctive cultural, ethnic, and economic settings.

Observations About Women's Preaching

The conviction that there is a distinctive quality to women's preaching is a conviction I have heard voiced in the community of homileticians within the United States. In the early stages of this research I wrote to ten professors of homiletics concerning a variety of issues related to women's preaching. The questions were broad and not necessarily related to feminism. The questions I raised all centered around the distinctive quality of women's preaching. I communicated with eight men and two women representing a geographical cross section of the country and a wide range of denominations. I am well aware of the limitations of such informal dialogue, yet I wish to share a few observations from those communications because they have continued to inspire my thinking about the direction, meaning, and vision of preaching done from a feminist perspective. These exchanges, coupled with my own observations of women's preaching for well over a decade, have helped me clarify the issues to be identified and articulated.

The professors with whom I communicated each affirmed that there is a definite distinctive quality to women's preaching. They also noted the difficulty in naming the specific dimensions of this distinctiveness. Within their overarching agreement the following observations were made:

> The sermons that I have heard in my classes as preached by women are generally better crafted and delivered than those preached by men. Perhaps women try harder, but in

addition to that I believe that women have better verbal
skills and use more imagination in their preaching.[2]

As a general rule, I would say that women tend to be more
creative and imaginative in dealing with the text, although
they sometimes are also more argumentative. I do feel that
women are only now beginning to identify some models for
preaching. Until very recently most of my women students
suffered from trying to imitate male models, and not always
good ones at that. With regard to gender-related difference,
the women are more inclusive in their use of language,
images, and illustrations. Their preaching tends to be, at
the same time, more imaginative and more relevant.[3]

These observations urge us to look at women's use of language in the preaching task as well as the role of imagination
as it influences the creativity and relevancy of women's preaching. The lack of clear female role models and the dominance of
male models of preacher still persist, providing two additional
reasons that feminist research in the field is so necessary.

I find in teaching that women tend to be more relational
and contextual in their preaching than men are, which
reflects our experience and the work currently being done
in women's psychology. I think we also are inclined to
direct our sermons to the person, rather than to the mind,
of the hearer.[4]

In this observation the question of intimacy and relationality
in women's preaching arises. We are pointed to the field of
women's psychology as a resource for further investigation and
understanding. This professor's response also suggests that
women preach in a more holistic way, addressing the whole
person rather than engaging the intellect alone.

Women use more images and more stories. Men use more
exegetical development. The texts women choose are less
abstract and more related to everyday, real-life issues.
Women use the imperative sparingly. Women are almost
always more self-revealing than men, and more consis-

tently begin with the contemporary experience and move to the text rather than moving from text to experience.[5]

As a teacher of preaching, and as a woman preacher, I use the image of weaving a great deal in my sermons. Women have a greater awareness of the interconnectedness of the personal level to the social justice level. Women are much more communal and have higher degrees of self-disclosure. There are a vast number of feminist influences shaping the nature of women's preaching today, and our understanding of spirituality in general.[6]

These observations invite us to look at women's use of imagery and raise initial questions about authority and women's preaching. The interconnectedness of life issues for women as well as the complexity of influences on women's spiritual and religious life raise important theological considerations for homiletics. These observations, although more general in nature about women's preaching, helped me discern key issues in the development of a view of preaching from a feminist perspective.

The Resource of Women's Sermons

Despite the significant absence of feminist theoretical work as it applies to women's preaching, several published collections of women's sermons served as a resource for my study. They are the following: *Women and the Word—Sermons,*[7] *Spinning a Sacred Yarn: Women Speak from the Pulpit,*[8] *Those Preachin' Women: Sermons by Black Women Preachers,*[9] and *Women of the Word: Contemporary Sermons by Women Clergy.*[10] I searched each of these volumes for explicit weaving images and metaphors as well as feminist theological thought and insight. Although several sermons describe "the tapestry of life," the warp and woof of life and faith, and the interwoven oneness of creation, in the majority of them weaving is more implicit than explicit.

Charles D. Hackett, in his introduction to *Women of the Word,* observes the following about the sermons contained in this collection of sermons by Anglican women:

In an entirely unexpected way, perhaps we are given a clue
about why each of these women seems to tell stories so well.
Perhaps we catch a glimpse of one aspect of the "female
experience." Throughout history, the story has belonged to
the disenfranchised and officially powerless. . . . The memo-
ries and hopes of conquered peoples without access to official means of communication are kept alive by sagas,
ritual remembrances, and stories.[11]

In all four collections of sermons the quality of "story" is
pervasive in nearly all of the sermons. It appears that many
women use story for two purposes: to name reality from a
woman's perspective and to serve as a means of self-disclosure.
I believe that for women, story and narrative theology are more
than a means of effective theologizing or a type of imaginative
communication. Story and narrative theologizing represent a
powerful and important way of naming reality for women, and
naming is clearly a critical feminist issue. Women have relied on
oral tradition throughout time as a means of preserving their
"herstory" and remembering their identities as women.

Another quality of many of the sermons is that, rather than
tell people what to do, women invite persons to reflect upon
their lives and the nature of their faith commitments. The exception to this may be the more imperative mode found in Black
women's preaching, as illustrated in the collection *Those
Preachin' Women.* I attribute this, however, to the distinctive
quality of Black preaching and the distinctive role and authority
Black preachers have within their religious communities. The
contrast between sermons written by white women preachers
and those written by Black women preachers might well serve
as a point of departure for future discussions about authority
and women's preaching.

The sermons in all four collections are rich in imagery, poetic language, and personal illustrations from women's lives.
In many of these sermons there is an interwoven quality that
integrates personal story, creative and imaginative language,
and imagery rooted in female experience. There is a pervasive
indicative mode, an increased sensitivity to inclusive language
and God imagery, and many explicit illustrations from female

experience in the world. Themes of oppression, suffering, and pain are also points of strong emphasis throughout these volumes. Some of the qualities exemplified in these volumes help us delineate and name distinctive feminist strands in the preaching craft.

Weaving as Primary Image and Metaphor

Women often look to images in order to name their own experiences and the life realities of women around them. In my attempt to articulate the "unnamed" realities about white Protestant women's preaching, I have found that the metaphor of weaving continues to describe for me the gathering of these distinctive qualities. Weaving is an image not simply of actuality but of possibility. Weaving does not merely describe the way preaching *is,* but it points in the direction of what feminist preaching is *coming to be.* It is not just descriptive; it is imaginative. The image of weaving is expansive and visionary, suggesting ways the world might be seen, the Christian faith proclaimed, the faithful life lived. It is an image that has limitless ways of affirming and proclaiming wholeness and integration in the life of faith. Weaving ultimately points to justice in the world because this image has at its heart the interlacing of conflict and struggle with vision and hope. I choose weaving, not because it is a romanticized image of the Christian life, but because weaving is a strong, powerful image that ultimately embodies the wholeness it suggests.

In recent years the craft of weaving itself has moved more into the realm of possibility and imagination, even though for many women around the world, weaving remains necessary for survival.

> Today, perhaps as a kind of protest to the busy, mechanized, and regulated world that we live in, people of all ages and interests are turning to handicrafts. We weave not so much from the necessity of making cloth to cover us or to beautify our surroundings, as from the human need to create something from raw materials. Weaving becomes an aesthetic exercise, instead of a domestic chore.[12]

For many women and men, weaving suggests a transforming and prophetic vision not only for change in their own personal lives but also for radical change in the world. Even though weaving appears to be for the most part explored, expressed, and affirmed by women, the spirit of justice and human wholeness at the heart of weaving is of universal human concern.

Weaving as Vision

Spinning and weaving for ages have symbolized in a powerful way the connections women have to the earth, to the cycles of life and death, and to female power and creativity. These connections as well as the profound wisdom that women have gained as a result of their weaving-work and experiences have emerged as foundational truths for feminist spirituality. In recent years weaving has become the central image and metaphor in my self-understanding as a pastor, preacher, and sacramental theologian. As a preacher, weaving represents a very particular kind of interwoven vision that informs both the content and style of my proclamations. Weaving ultimately suggests a way of life.

In 1986 I created an art piece that combined images of women weaving with women's poetry and women's music. The intent of the created work was to demonstrate how broadly the image of weaving is reflected in women's lives today and to make more explicit my own understanding of weaving as a visionary metaphor for living faithfully in the contemporary world. A portion of the script follows:

> To weave is to spin . . . to sew . . . to birth a new reality bringing together what once was separate . . . a creation of the hands, the soul, the mind, working together to form a tapestry . . . rich with color . . . texture . . . and meaning. Weaving . . . spinning . . . web-building . . . are ways of living . . . ways of living sacramentally . . . forms of worship. Weaving is a form of consciousness where ordinary distinctions between the self and others vanish, as do distinctions between one subject and another. All is seen as one whole, wherein not only is everything part of everything else; ev-

erything *is* everything else. The vision from which weaving emerges proclaims that we and our environment are an interwoven fabric in which every strand crosses every other. When we corrupt it, we corrupt ourselves, because in reality the two cannot be separated.

> Spinsters . . . weavers . . . web-builders . . . spin and weave, mending and creating unity of consciousness . . . spanning all false dichotomies . . . knowing that the same energy that gives life creates oneness . . . bringing together those things that too long have been separate . . . body and spirit . . . earth and human life . . . sacred and ordinary . . . age and youth . . . creating and making plain a vision of wholeness, as weaving crashes through boundaries of conditioning . . . lies . . . false images . . . and separateness.

Weaving as Craft

As I moved more deeply into implications and insights of weaving for my own religious self-understanding and my discernment of the preaching task, I decided to learn how to weave. Learning how to weave on a loom deromanticized all my preconceived ideas. It is a difficult and intricate craft, demanding great patience and detailed work. The craft involves a constant balance between technical skills and personal creativity. It is the combination of finely developed skills and creative vision that makes a weaving a truly artistic creation and a weaver an excellent artisan.

> The weaver must not only understand the mechanics of the loom and the techniques of weave construction but must also judge what arrangement of visual elements will best express his [her] intentions and interpret his [her] vision. Many artists apply the "rules" of design instinctively and naturally . . . : they have been reviewed, absorbed, discarded, and broken in every epoch of art according to the individual needs of the artist and age.[13]

Learning how to weave has affirmed for me the truth that in any craft, be it weaving or preaching, one must balance structure and creativity, principles of design and form with imagination and vision. It is not merely the vision and symbolic message of weaving that influence and inform the preacher; the technical and practical aspects of the weaving craft also shed light on preaching method and style.

Learning to weave deepened my appreciation of weaving as an image that adequately embodies the vision of wholeness and connectedness that is central to the lives and ministries of many feminist women. Seeing weaving as a way of life at the center of one's spirituality and at the heart of one's preaching requires the capacity and commitment to make connections. One is called to see one's own unique life tapestry as fundamentally and intimately related and interwoven with the tapestries of all others. It is the vision that these distinctive human tapestries might coexist in mutual respect and solidarity that produces for our world hope for increasing harmony, deep pervasive peace, and inclusive justice. It is not that human distinctions disappear; it is rather that the distinctions are interwoven together in such a way as to enhance both the separateness of each strand and the woven texture of the whole.

Deepening Insights Into Weaving

My understanding of the vision and craft of weaving has been deepened and expanded by feminist literature, visual art, music, and feminist spirituality resources. I am indebted to Native American culture and wisdom for my initial and ongoing belief in weaving as a visionary metaphor for life. My first important exposure to the craft of weaving came through the Cherokee basket weavers of North Carolina and Tennessee. I next developed an interest in the rugs and weavings of Navajo weavers of the Southwest. As my exposure to various types of weaving expanded, so did my understanding of it as an image and vision for faithful living. This ever-expanding vision of life and faith has stretched me into deeper understandings of connection, integration, wholeness, and interwoven unity. When I began to read Native American poetry and literature and explore the spiritual wisdom of several Native American tribes, vision and craft became one.

In the myths of the Pueblo people, Spider Woman created the world and then taught her people how to weave threads and their lives into beautiful tapestries. She is seen as their mother, their grandmother, their friend and teacher, and a powerful mystery in their midst.[14] She is a female deity who embodies and symbolizes strength, creativity, and unity. Many women and men who stand outside a Native American heritage are only beginning to appreciate the ancient wisdom of these native people. Native Americans view spiders as sacred weavers. Out of their very beginnings spiders spin strands that become majestic webs, webs that merge heaven and earth, blade of grass to blade of grass, window edge to window edge. They deliberately span environments with intense energy and work. They give birth to threads of connectedness, somehow creating out of their own bodies a substance that will bring together separate edges, walls, and space. The connection between web building and weaving is profound; the cloth that is formed from weaving is called a web.

> Warp threads run lengthwise of the loom. Back and forth, across these tightly stretched threads, a shuttle is passed carrying the weft threads. The interlocking of these two sets of threads forms what is called the cloth or web.[15]

Spiders and weavers remind us that to live out of our own integrity as women and men and to base our spirituality and practice of ministry on that integrity demand that we confront and span dichotomies that split, divide, and destroy the world. This "web-weaving" wisdom challenges us to live on the boundary of what is safe, known, and secure in order to spin and weave a new reality.

Weaving and Preaching

Worship and preaching moments that spin and weave a new reality of justice and human wholeness, and those that push us to live on the boundary, are the proclamations that have integrity and meaning for contemporary living. Justice and human wholeness are embodied in our proclamations both in content and style. The spirit of our Creator moves us to make deeper and

broader connections with all creation. Preaching must help us
make these connections. It must empower us to sustain the work
and intentionality which those webs of connection demand, and
strengthen us to develop increasing clarity about the systems,
forces, and structures in our world that must be dismantled if
we are to weave the new. Preaching as an act of weaving demands that preachers be prophetic in their confrontations,
hopeful in their voices of vision.

The beauty and vision of weaving demand a response. If we
allow the transforming vision of weaving to come into the center
of our lives, we must in turn be weavers of justice and wholeness
in our world. Appreciation is only a preface to action.

One preacher speaks about his indebtedness to the women's
community for the image of weaving as an organizing metaphor
in his own understanding of preaching:

> For me the image which begins to get at the type of truth
> which good preaching embodies is the image of weaving.
> I am indebted to feminism for this image, and more
> specifically, to Adrienne Rich who speaks in one of her
> poems of discovering an old piece of a grandmother's
> patchwork, never finished, and of taking up the work where
> the grandmother had left off. . . . A true sermon is a
> tapestry drawn from tradition, memory, conversations long
> forgotten, candor, courtesy, pain and passion, fresh insight
> and fresh metaphor, but all united.[16]

The Guiding Essence

Both the vision of weaving and the skills of the weaving craft
itself have fundamentally shaped my work in the development
of weaving as a metaphor for preaching from a feminist perspective. There are additional crafts that women do which are
equally visionary. In an article entitled "Needle and Thread
Warriors," Marjorie Agosin writes about arpilleras, which are
small wall hangings depicting the everyday oppressive experiences and realities of life in Chile. These hangings are created
to generate economic resources for survival and to speak a

powerful word of truth and protest. These arpilleras represent the deepest yearnings of the women who create them.

> Each arpillera is a small scene from the life of the woman who creates it; just as their lives have been torn into pieces, the arpillera also consists of scraps of left-over material, put together slowly and in sorrow. . . . The group of women that began making arpilleras in 1974 were also members of the Association of Families of Detained-Disappeared. . . . These arpilleras of brightly colored scraps speak of pain and hope. . . . The women who make them use their pain to try to forge a just society for all. . . . This is the feminine form of political action where personal power is not the goal, but collective power is sought because it is perceived as the only instrument of change.[17]

The image of the arpillera is a powerful statement indeed! Similar in vision to a weaving, these needlework expressions represent the collective work of women in Chile working to support their families while at the same time bearing political witness against an oppressive government. For many women the skill and act of tapestry making is born of necessity, yet these creations make powerful statements about hope and justice.

Whether a woman weaves a shirt in Guatemala, a basket in Africa, or a Navajo rug in the United States, the craft of weaving always involves the process of uniting and integrating separate strands into an interwoven whole. Sometimes the weaving depicts real-life situations and experiences in a very explicit way within the weaving itself, while at other times the very interwoven nature of the weaving portrays a vision of unity and wholeness. There are countless methods, styles, and types of weaving, but the essence of the craft is that it always involves the process of uniting and integrating separate strands into an interwoven whole. Let us now examine the separate strands of female cultural experience, feminist theological critique, the vision of global feminism, and feminist issues in style and method as they unite into a metaphor of integration and wholeness for feminist preaching.

2

Weaver:
Woman as Preacher

When we become weavers, our efforts form part of the modern link in the long chain of weaving history that dates back 20,000 years or more. . . . As with all crafts, a certain amount of patience is required, but patience will grow and relaxation settle in as you build up your skills and become intrigued with the interplay of color, the texture of yarns, and the beauty and logic of fabric construction. . . . Unless you are weaving under a deadline, whether you are slow or fast does not matter. What does matter is the amount of enjoyment and fascination you find in the delight of "doing." This "doing" is a constantly revitalizing process, for, as you watch the woven article develop on your loom, new ideas and endless possibilities for further exploration open up before you.[1]

I believe that many women see and experience preaching as a profound act of human connection and intimacy. The first question a woman may ask herself is a fundamental one about how she will weave her life together with the lives of others in the preaching act. When the preacher is a woman, there are several basic realities brought to the task that will give shape to the relational dynamic in her preaching: distinctive female life experiences, female human development, and the particular relational understandings and commitments women embrace.

Feminist theologians, ethicists, historians, and biblical scholars continue to confront the church with the truth that women bring to their disciplines a distinctive experience and a particular voice of truth. The same assertion is equally important in the field of homiletics. Women bring to the preaching craft a different worldview and experience that inform and expand the ways preachers see themselves. Many scholars in the fields of psychology and sociology contend that women understand and experience intimacy and relatedness in gender-specific ways. These insights may illumine more fully the ways women understand relationships and power, deepening and broadening our vision of the particular weaver who undertakes the craft of preaching.

In this chapter I am drawing heavily on the scholarly work of women's psychology to draw insights about intimacy, relatedness, and female experience in women's preaching. There are other fields of literature from which one might receive insights into who the preacher is as woman, but women's psychology has been particularly evocative for me as I try to clarify and articulate my own female experience and understand the life experiences of other contemporary women. There also exists a significant body of literature in the field of women's psychology that makes a comparative study of several major writers in the field possible. This literature reflects profound similarities in women's experiences of reality and articulates the ramifications of common enculturation.

I acknowledge the difference between this chapter on women's psychology and the rest of the book. In chapters 1, 3, 4, and 5, the focus of my research is on the explicit connection between feminist theology, feminist vision, feminist imagery and metaphors, and an understanding of and participation in the preaching craft. In this chapter the insights from women's psychology are not always explicitly feminist in nature. This chapter clearly pertains to female experience in general, whereas the remaining chapters pertain to scholarship and commitments that are self-consciously feminist.

In several popular preaching texts, such as *Fundamentals of Preaching* by John Killinger, preachers are encouraged to immerse themselves in contemporary understandings of psychology, which provides a responsible resource for insights into human intimacy and communication.[2] These same books, however, do not mention the rich resource of women's psychology as a source for understanding human development and intimacy

more fully. Perhaps this failure to look at women's psychology
points to an unwillingness to question the blatant male naming
and defining of relatedness and intimacy. Traditional psycholo-
gists often support human divisions, individual autonomy, and
modes of relating that are built on levels of dominating power.
Women's psychology speaks about nonhierarchical modes of
relating, the connections between all created beings, and the
equal value of different gender development and experience.

Weaving Insights from Women's Psychology

Feminists within the church have known for some time that
hierarchy, special authority, and dominating power contribute
to woman's marginality and oppression as well as to the oppression of all that doesn't represent white male patriarchy. Yet with
the ever-growing knowledge and research of women's psychology and related fields, many women are now beginning to see
that hierarchy and separatedness are styles of relating to the
world that emerge mostly within male development and psychology. These styles of relating are in great contrast to female
development and reality and the distinctive ways in which
women tend to relate to others. While men, particularly white
men, appear to have autonomy, individuality, and detachment
as integral focus points in their development and growth,
women appear to have at the heart of their development qualities of affiliation and interconnectedness. Contemporary gender
research affirms that the developmental processes for women
and men are quite different and produce very different worldviews and life goals. One's worldview and life goals then influence one's understanding of authority and intimacy. Much has
been written in criticism of traditional models of authority and
their implications for intimacy, yet women theologians and
preachers are only now beginning to use as fully as we might the
data from women's psychology. These data enable a further
critique of hierarchical modes of relationality to be substan-
tiated from truths in human development. It is to that body of
wisdom I now turn in order to weave its truths into our present
understandings of intimacy as connectedness and mutuality.

Investigating the research and proposed conclusions of

women's psychology is an awesome task. I have not approached the literature with the intention to prove the inherent differences between females and males, nor has it been my desire to glean from it the basic distinctiveness of female and male personality traits and abilities. In my review of several main sources in women's psychology, it has become increasingly clear that the data are very indecisive and inconclusive about such differences. This is not to say that there are no differences; it is only to say that research still finds these differences difficult to define and their origins almost impossible to chart accurately. Carol Tavris and Carole Wade, in *The Longest War,* agree with this assertion:

> Differences in physical strength don't mean much. Differences in ability are minor. Differences in personality are elusive. But men and women do have different images of themselves and of how the world works; they seem to have different moral premises; they seem to regard conflict and choice from different directions.[3]

I approach this psychological scholarship in terms of what it reveals about women's experience and worldview, both of which have been silenced and made invisible by a patriarchal perspective that declares male to be normative. Women's psychology reveals to us that women's experience and self-understanding have direct bearing on issues of relatedness and intimacy, and thus on women and men's preaching. Ann Belford Ulanov, in *Receiving Woman,* articulates very clearly my purpose as I seek to integrate and weave the wisdom of women's psychology into my understandings about proclamation from a feminist perspective:

> The locus of authority now shifts for women. They must recognize themselves as no mere variations on the male. The symbolism of the feminine is more than a complementary part of masculine images, and both stand for a special way of being and becoming, each with its own impetus and direction. Such an approach may lead to the discovery of an abiding authority that issues from women's own experiences.[4]

The following summary of my research into women's psychology is an attempt to weave the dignity of women's experience, worldview, and relational commitments into a tapestry of real giftedness that begins to celebrate the distinctive quality of women's presence and self in the preaching act.

The body of knowledge in women's psychology is vast and complex, often detailed and technical. Because my focus is on intimacy and relationality in women's preaching rather than on psychology per se, I explore the most relevant assertions from women's psychology that apply to my topic. I will weave together the wisdom from women's psychology with my knowledge of the preaching task, drawing implications and conclusions about themes of intimacy, connectedness, authority, and solidarity where the two disciplines connect. Because I know of no research that attempts to draw connections between women's psychology and preaching, I have chosen to present the data from women's psychology in summary form, focused again on one major area of investigation—women's understanding of intimacy and women's sense of profound relationality. I will draw most extensively from the following four sources: Carol Gilligan's *In a Different Voice,* Nancy Chodorow's *The Reproduction of Mothering,* Luise Eichenbaum and Susie Orbach's *Understanding Women,* and Jean Baker Miller's *Toward a New Psychology of Women.*

One concern must be raised about the findings from this research. Because I am not trained in psychology, I raise this concern primarily out of my feminist consciousness. In many areas of feminist research and thought there is today a growing awareness that at times our research has been so motivated by the desire to "articulate women's experience" that we have failed to name and claim the particularities and limitations of our diversity. This is another form of oppression and one constantly perpetuated by white women of privilege. I am concerned that this same omission exists within the research and discipline of women's psychology. I am unclear and somewhat at a loss when I attempt to imagine how women of color, lesbian women, poor white women, and differently abled women might experience the findings from this predominantly white middle-class group of female theorists. I can only presume that their research is clearly biased in terms of class, race, ethnicity, physical privilege, and access. I share the observations and insights of this body of knowledge in feminist studies, aware of the limitations and hopeful that one day the particularities of all women's experience will be more fully explored and analyzed.

Understanding the Weaver's World: Intimacy and Relatedness

Intimacy is central to the way many women in our culture view and experience the world. There is consistent agreement within women's psychology that relatedness and attachment are at the heart and center of women's development and mode of being. Whether one describes women's reality as a web of connection,[5] a more complex relational constellation,[6] affiliation and attachment,[7] or merger and dependency,[8] all five authors whose work I have studied suggest the presence of a distinctive quality in regard to women's way of relating to the world. Across the literature, relational connectedness is central to women's life goals, vision of life, moral and ethical decision making, and experiences of self-worth and meaning.

Jean Baker Miller, a practicing psychotherapist, published *Toward a New Psychology of Women* in 1976. This was a very important contribution to the field because it endeavored to portray the distinctive gifts of female experience. The underlying motivation for the book was Miller's attempt to give expression to those distinctive qualities that are a part of women's experience and particular ways of viewing the world that had not previously been articulated or valued. One of her first assertions shows her passion for unmasking a greater vision of human potential by revealing the importance of women's perspective. "Humanity has been held to a limited and distorted view of itself—from its interpretation of the most intimate of personal emotions to its grandest vision of human possibilities—precisely by virtue of its subordination of women."[9]

Miller proceeds to chart women's subordination in our society, naming several key repercussions related to the domination of an entire class of people, women. She reminds us of a reality that is well known by feminists today but was not as widely asserted when the book appeared. Any dominant group inevitably controls the culture's overall outlook, its philosophy, morality standards, social theory, and its science. Ultimately, those who dominate will define the realities in a culture and assign the relative value. Because of the reality of women's subordination, qualities long associated with female experience have been devalued and made invisible. Miller offers a balance to this devaluing by naming various strengths of the female worldview, several of which pertain directly to intimacy: capacity to acknowledge feelings of vulnerability and weakness; recognition of cooperation as an essential human value; centrality of affiliation and attachment in women's basic life experience; and responsiveness to the needs of others.[10]

> Women, both superficially and deeply, are more closely in touch with basic life experiences—in touch with reality. . . . Emotionality, as part and parcel of every state of being, is even more pervasive than feelings of vulnerability and weakness. In our dominant tradition, however, it has not been seen as an aid to understanding and action, but rather as an impediment, even an evil.[11]

Vulnerability and Emotionality

At the risk of confirming traditional female stereotypes, Miller affirms the knowledge and experience many women seem to possess about feelings of vulnerability and emotionality. I was reminded, while reading her redefinitions and affirmations of women's experience, that the valuing of such experience or knowledge lies totally within the power control of a white male system of thought and experience. In such a system of domination, it is essential for women to assert their own power to name and to claim the value of their distinctive female experience. This is not a matter of luxury, nor merely an academic or scholarly venture; it is a matter of the survival of the self for most women. The very existence of the discipline of women's psychology confronts us with the reality that female development and experience have until only recently been viewed as tangential to the norm. Why has vulnerability and emotionality been viewed as something in our culture which must be suppressed? How would our experience of intimacy change were we to value the expression of feelings more than we value control and distance?

Cooperation

Coupled with a willingness to admit vulnerability and emotionality, Miller asserts that women tend to view cooperation in a way fundamentally different from the way the dominant white male culture does. "Another important aspect of women's psychology is women's greater recognition of the essential cooperative nature of human existence,"[12] she says. Women are much less likely to view cooperation as potential loss of self and power and are much more able to affirm it as a necessity for basic human solidarity and cooperation. For many men, particularly white males whose basic male experience is rooted in autonomy and individuation, cooperation holds within it a basic threat, the loss of individual identity. One need only look at the structuring of white patriarchal society to identify which quality has dominated our human interaction. Can we learn from women's experience a new appreciation for the essential cooperative nature of relatedness? How would intimacy change were we to value cooperation and coexistence more than autonomy?

Affiliation and Attachment

The centrality of affiliation and attachment as well as women's responsiveness to the needs of others form the focus of Miller's final analysis of women's strengths and life experiences of intimacy:

> One central feature is that women stay with, build on, and develop in a context of attachment and affiliation with others . . . affiliation is valued . . . more than self-enhancement. Women can be highly developed and still give great weight to affiliations.[13]

The capacity to affiliate and to attend responsively to the needs of others is a critical aspect of human intimacy. Perhaps female experience may shed new light on how human beings might balance the goals of self-enhancement and relatedness so that they are interwoven dimensions of relational life instead of competing visions. Can it be that female experience might confront a patriarchal worldview with the possibility of self-enhancement *within* affiliation and attachment? How would intimacy change were we to value attachment and responsiveness more than individual self-enhancement?

It is important to interject a word of caution. It is not the idolizing of women's experience that is needed; rather it is equal valuing and the recognition that in order to take female experience seriously our common understandings of human relational life must radically change. In a system dominated by white male experience, it is very clear that the idolizing of these aspects of women's experience has only served to solidify and absolutize the oppressive stereotyping of women. An equal valuing of the female experience of intimacy that allows for all people to embrace greater intimacy takes seriously the wisdom of this distinctive experience for the entire human community's understanding of human intimacy.

My commitment lies in the integration and interweaving of female experience into the dominant culture's worldview in such a way that the dominant culture is transformed. Thus, to name the dangers honestly in celebrating distinctive female understandings of intimacy, to know and recognize the possible ways the illumination of female experience might be distorted and abused, is absolutely essential. Despite Miller's basic focus on naming and affirming the distinctiveness of female experience, she is aware of the oppressive nature of exclusive female stereotyping, and the inherent human need for balance and integration.

Vulnerability and emotionality are powerful issues within intimacy when they are interwoven with a strong sense of self and a sense of one's power in the world to respond and to act. Often women have distinctive knowledge from their female experience, yet have very little power to assert that knowledge in the world. Cooperation appears to be something about which women know a great deal. Ironically, this seems to be true for many reasons, not the least of which is the powerlessness of women within the structures of a patriarchal society. For women, cooperation is both something we value and something we recognize to be quite necessary for our survival. The word *solidarity* reminds us that cooperation is a quality embodied by equal partners who share a common vision and task. Cooperation cannot be built on the weakness of any of the members. Too frequently women have been forced, and sometimes have chosen, to collapse themselves into cooperation rather than assert themselves in freely chosen solidarity.

Finally, the centrality of affiliation, attachment, and responsiveness to the needs of others has its dangers for women. Intimacy is rooted in the mutual valuing of one for another. It affirms the basic worth of each person's selfhood. Women, conditioned to be caretakers and experts in sensitivity, too often know of no other avenue to real intimacy than by means of their constant caring and their caretaking skills rather than by their independent self-worth. Affiliation too often produces in women a loss of ego boundaries and a weakened sense of self. The life-giving dimension to female affiliation and responsiveness emerges when women choose relatedness as a primary value in their lives and an expression of a strong sense of self rather than as a means to create and sustain a sense of self-worth and identity.

Even amid the dangers, these strengths of the female worldview have much to offer the development of future definitions, understandings, and experiences of intimacy and connectedness in our culture, and in our preaching. They now are influencing the fundamental questions of culture that are beginning to be raised about the nature and importance of intimacy in the human community. "As women start to define these new principles [of their own valuable qualities] for themselves they emphasize different issues and questions."[14] These new questions and issues will eventually move us all to new realities.

Nancy Chodorow's *The Reproduction of Mothering: The Psychoanalysis and the Sociology of Gender,* published in 1978, sheds additional light on the topic of women and intimacy as she systematically explores the question of gender identity in relation to the institution of mothering in our culture. Her analysis, clearly from the perspective of a sociologist, revolves around a rather sophisticated understanding of the sociology of culture and gender. From her technical and scholarly work, the most poignant insights for my exploration of women and their understandings and experiences of intimacy will be drawn.

Chodorow's basic assertion can be stated most effectively in her own words, "Girls and boys develop different relational capacities and senses of self as a result of growing up in a family in which women mother."[15] Her analysis of gender differences focuses entirely on the phenomenon of females as the primary parents and caretakers of children in our society, and the results of that cultural reality.

Female/Male Development

The main portion of her research is devoted to exploring specific female and male development in a system where women mother. Her analysis is rooted in object-relations theory best described again in Chodorow's words: "Object-relations theorists argue that the child's social relational experience from earliest infancy is determining for psychological growth and personality formation."[16] More specifically in terms of gender differences and issues of relatedness, the fact that children are primarily parented by women becomes *determinative* in how those children will formulate and understand human intimacy.

Chodorow charts in much detail the states of psychological development through which girls and boys move in their growth toward adulthood. The final results are very different understandings of, and skills for, human intimacy. She expands and transforms Freudian concepts, uprooting them from their exclusive male bias, and attempts to reveal what happens to females and males in their early development of gender identity. A synopsis of this development and its primary impact on understandings of intimacy and human solidarity follows:

> Because of their mothering by women, girls come to experience themselves as less separate than boys, as having more permeable ego boundaries. Girls seem to define themselves more in relation to others.[17]

Mothers are clearer about their son's differences, thus mothers push differentiation. Boys finally replace mother and their attachment with father, and choose the superiority of masculine identification.[18] In a society where women mother, girls do not experience themselves as other, nor are they detached from mother the same ways boys differentiate themselves. A boy's masculinity depends on his *detachment,* a girl's femininity on her *attachment.* From the very beginning, a different relational reality forms for girls than for boys. Even when girls identify with father and move toward their fathers for attachment and affirmation, their mothers remain primary, both emotionally and relationally.

This is a major departure from traditional Freudian analysis of female development. Girls do not break away from mother, but rather add a relationship with father. These developmental years produce differing "relational potential" for girls and boys, potential that permeates adulthood. Boys emerge defining themselves as separate and distinct, with a greater sense of differentiation and clearer ego boundaries. The masculine sense of self is separate; the basic feminine sense of self is connected to the world. "From the stage of the . . . oedipus complex and its resolution, women's endo-psychic object-world becomes a more complex relational constellation than men's, and women remain preoccupied with ongoing relational issues . . . in a way that men do not."[19]

Because women mother in our culture, boys learn otherness and detachment; girls learn identification and bonding. Girls appear to integrate intimacy with father into the pattern of intimacy already established with mother, producing a complex relational pattern in female development. Boys appear to break away from mother, attempt to identify and attach to father, whose masculine differentiation doesn't allow for such attachments, ultimately producing a pattern of separateness, autonomy, and detachment in boys' male development. This developmental patterning makes a radical difference in adult female and male capacities for and commitments to intimacy and connectedness.

The clarity and power with which Chodorow illumines the

primary impact of women's mothering on gender differences and relational potential is evocative and profound. She opens traditional psychological theory and concepts and claims a female perspective within these exclusive categories. Her final objective may be to make clear the limitations and ultimate losses caused when parenting is exclusively done by females. Human development is unbalanced, and gender differences are stereotypically reinforced.

One may conclude that in a system where both females and males act as primary caretakers, women would develop stronger self-identity and differentiation, and men would develop stronger capacities for intimacy and relatedness. Until that vision becomes reality, Chodorow's analysis illumines new understandings into the distinctive gender differences surrounding intimacy and connectedness that are so apparent yet so difficult to name and understand. Whereas Jean Baker Miller begins to describe and articulate the particularities of women's universal experience of being female, Chodorow provides a more detailed analysis of a specific cultural phenomenon in women's lives. Her work supports and develops Miller's, supplying concrete documentation and explanation for Miller's assertions. Chodorow is concerned with the analysis of structures that determine female life experience; Miller is concerned with the analysis of individual psychological development.

Carol Gilligan, in her ground-breaking book *In a Different Voice: Psychological Theory and Women's Development,* provides yet another distinctive approach to female development and growth. Operating within the field of developmental psychology, she is highly critical of traditional psychology for its blatant disregard of women's perspectives, commitments, and distinctive worldviews. Her particular contribution is the critique and analysis of moral and ethical developmental theories.

Traditional Moral Development

Traditional developmental theories have based their conclusions on observation of men's lives, with minimal or no attention to women's distinctive gender differences. Not only has traditional moral and ethical development been focused on male values and norms while systematically ignoring the same development in females, but the theories have served to create and perpetuate female inequality, oppression, and inferior stereotyping. Women constantly are measured against a system of development that is in disharmony with their basic life experience and psychological growth.

Using the data from three extensive studies, Gilligan describes and delineates the distinctively different mode of making moral and ethical decisions that she found in the female population she studied. The focus of her research is on the discovery of a distinctive female voice, a voice of particular truths and life perceptions that has not been adequately understood and valued in our male-dominated culture. "The disparity between women's experience and the representation of human development, noted throughout the psychological literature, has generally been seen to signify a problem in women's development. Instead, the failure of women to fit existing models of human growth may point to a problem in the representation, a limitation in the conception of human condition, an omission of certain truths about life."[20] Her study spanned a ten-year period during which she began to notice two differences in the voices of women and men: (1) there were two different modes of speaking about moral and ethical problems, and (2) the modes of describing the relationship between self and other were gender-distinctive.[21] Upon noticing these different modes of viewing the world of decision making and the arenas of human relationships, she constructs an inclusive developmental theory that takes seriously the voice of women.

Distinct Female Development

Gilligan initially draws from the work of Nancy Chodorow, describing the need for male children to separate and differentiate while female children's self-identity is not formulated on individuation and separation. This developmental scheme leaves males feeling threatened about intimacy, and females about separation and individuation. As a portion of her larger feminist critique of traditional developmental theory, Gilligan suggests that the result of traditional development is destructive to full

and balanced human wholeness. As with Miller's and Chodorow's research, Gilligan makes no naive assumption that these
differences are equally valued in our society, but points to the
negative valuing of female ethical and moral development while
male development is seen as normative.

In the area of relationships, Gilligan reminds us that women's
experience of relatedness continues to be the most unexplored,
mysterious area of psychological exploration.[22] In each of her
three studies—the first, a college study about identity; the second, an abortion study examining experience, thought, and the
nature of conflict; and the third, a study on rights and responsibilities focused on morality and views of self—the interviewed
females consistently and overwhelmingly gave answers reflecting a very complex network of relational commitments, values,
and perspectives. Gilligan discovered that women's sense of self
is clearly organized around being able to make and maintain
affiliations and relationships. This sense of self, however, is seriously threatened in a culture that encourages detachment and
autonomy. "When the interconnections of the web are dissolved
by the hierarchical ordering of relationships, when nets are
portrayed as dangerous entrapments, impeding flight rather
than protecting against fall, women come to question whether
what they have seen exists and whether what they know from
their own experience is true."[23] Women tend to experience relatedness like a web of interconnections, all of which are important
and essential to a meaningful and full life. A woman's sense of
self is rooted in this web of relationships, sometimes to her own
disadvantage when she seeks to develop a strong sense of self
and a strong, independent voice of her own.

Moral and ethical issues and decisions, absolute judgments,
abstract moralizing, rigid decision-making processes, and the
supremacy of individual rights, all yield for women to the all-
pervasive power of relationships. Women tend to consider ethical decisions in relation to responsibilities and networks of
relationships. Men tend to think in terms of rights and self-
enhancement. Women will most often speak in terms of the care
of all people involved and the maintenance of connection. Men
will most often speak of the need to respect others' rights and
the quest for self-fulfillment in the midst of ethical and moral

dilemmas. Interdependence and the ethics of care and responsibility become the foundational modes of female decision making. Autonomy and the capacity to make individual decisions based on abstract rights and truths become the foundational modes of male decision making.

There are feminist voices today that dispute this very assumption of Gilligan. They contend that feminist ethical decision making is often based on the objective, normative concept of justice. Gilligan does, in fact, fail to suggest that there might be norms for ethical and moral behavior that are absolutely normative for women. Her focus on description and documentation of the importance of the relationality of women's lives leads her work to suggest that women have no normative standards by which they make decisions. Relationality needs further explanation and development in order to take into account such substantive norms as justice—a norm, I suggest, that permeates the heart and task of feminist vision, critique, and methodology. Although Gilligan's work is a major contribution to feminist studies, her categories must be viewed through a critical feminist lens. Relationality cannot be equated necessarily with mutuality, solidarity, and justice—ultimate points of valuing for feminism.

Intimacy and Connectedness

As one may easily conclude from Gilligan's study, intimacy and connectedness are absolutely primary in the life cycle of females and are significantly present in all ethical decision making. "Thus in all of the women's descriptions, identity is defined in a context of relationship and judged by a standard of responsibility and care."[24] When women construct the adult domain, the world of relationships emerges and becomes the focus of attention and concern. This is not to suggest that individuation and separation are not also needed aspects of psychological development for women. A healthy balance is most surely necessary. Rather, these findings suggest, as did Miller's and Chodorow's, that women bring to the world a distinctive way of valuing human relatedness and intimacy. This highly developed commitment to connection and to interdependence is a portion of women's development and way of being in a world that has never been significantly valued by a culture constructed on the truths and values of male development. Here are tremendous and obvious implications for the ways in which all human beings might view relational intimacy and connectedness, and assent to its central importance for the sustaining of life.

My exploration of insights about intimacy in women's psychology ends with a brief summary of poignant insights from Luise Eichenbaum and Susie Orbach's book *Understanding Women: A Feminist Psychoanalytic Approach.* Their work is a compilation of the insights and discoveries of two women psychotherapists regarding the construction of a feminine psychology. A large portion of the book explores the struggles women face in therapy in order to become whole, integrated human beings. Throughout the book is found a serious and persistent critique of the patriarchal context in which women develop. The book identifies and articulates a number of obstacles that women must overcome as a result of this pervasive patriarchal domination if they are to become independent women. Unlike Miller, Chodorow, and Gilligan, whose main focus is to illumine the development and creation of a distinctive female mode of relating and forming intimacy, Eichenbaum and Orbach delve more deeply into the distortions of intimacy many women must redefine and overcome in order to experience the fullness of human relatedness.

In a patriarchal society there are clear psychological demands placed on women: the demand to defer to others and a subsequent lack of recognition of one's own sense of self-worth; the demand always to be connected to another and the resultant impact of shaping one's life always according to another person, most often a man; the demand to have emotional antennae and the constant challenge to anticipate others' needs.[25] These expectations are clearly passed from mothers to daughters and, for most girls, internalized as a normal part of early childhood development. Because mothers and daughters share gender identity, social role, and social expectations, often there is a very unclear sense of differentiation within this primary relationship. Mothers tend to overidentify with daughters, often projecting onto daughters their own feelings about self and engaging in confusing behaviors that encourage their daughter's independence while simultaneously communicating dependence expectations. This first and primary relationship in the daughter's life remains central to the girl's entire developmental process.

"Just as mother responds to and anticipates the needs of others, and just as mother identifies with the yearnings and needs of others, so the daughter comes to embody this same capacity for giving."[26] Perhaps the greatest distortion of intimacy in early female development is the all-powerful message that one is to be caretaker, total nurturer, and servant to all. Because mothers have often been the victims of this patriarchal expectation, they consciously and unconsciously pass this expectation on to their daughters. These expectations of who and what women will be as caretakers often leaves many women themselves feeling uncared for and very dependent.

Within the psychotherapy relationship, as Eichenbaum and Orbach explain and detail the stages, women learn how to work through their own dependency and thus transform their understandings and experiences of intimacy. In a therapeutic relationship, women are provided with enough support, a trusting and safe environment, and the encouragement of a woman therapist so as to enable their growing separateness while valuing their knowledge and perceptions of intimacy and life commitments to relatedness.

Eichenbaum and Orbach say: "The fabric of intimacy is woven of three elements: boundaries, dependency, and separateness."[27] Women often know a great deal about dependency and connectedness, and are challenged in therapy to develop clearer ego boundaries and a well-defined sense of self that exists apart from others yet is related in intimate ways to others. The therapeutic process becomes the arena where women have their female experience validated, their commitments to a complex web of relationships affirmed, their underdeveloped self and boundaries strengthened, and their needs and ability to merge and separate clarified.

Eichenbaum and Orbach conclude with an observation and affirmation similar to that of Chodorow's: Men must become primary caregivers in our culture. As long as women remain the exclusive caretakers of children and fathers are detached, daughters and sons will receive some very distorted and limited views of intimacy, boundaries, and self-identity.

The Weaver: Woman as Preacher

The insights about female experience, enculturation, and worldview need to be woven into homiletical thought and practice. Thus far, the discipline reflects only the perspective and wisdom of male experience in general, and white male experience in particular. When the preacher is a woman, perhaps there is a radically different relational understanding at work in the act of proclamation. This difference suggests to us that women preachers feel that the relationship established in the moment of preaching is as crucial to life and faith as the truths of the biblical witness. In sharp contrast to traditional expectations of the preacher's role, if preaching is fundamentally a relational act, preachers also need to bring the fullness of who they are to the task.

The reality of female experience, women's self-identity, and women's sense of intimacy and relatedness in the world are central to the weaver/preacher. I understand the beginning point for women's weaving/preaching to be basic female experience and being. Even though this basic female experience will take countless forms and shapes and be expressed in infinite styles and ways, a part of the weaving/preaching of all women is their foundational experience of being female. If a woman is Chicana, Filipino, lesbian, Black, or differently abled, her female experience becomes increasingly complex in its particularity; the experience of being female is always present in the very structure and reality of her human existence. It is this reality of female experience and all of its particularities that provide the basic self-identity out of which women weave their preaching creation. It is this basic female wisdom and worldview that imbues women's preaching with its own distinctive quality and power. Julia Esquivel, in her poem "Indian Tapestry," celebrates the power and distinctive reality of the weaver in these words:

When I go up to the house of the Old Weaver,
I watch in admiration
at what comes forth from her mind:
a thousand designs being created
and not a single model from which to copy
the marvelous cloth
with which she will dress
the companion of the True and Faithful One.

Men always ask me
to give the name of the label,
to specify the maker of the design.
But the Weaver cannot be pinned down
by designs,
or patterns.
All of her weavings
are originals,
there are no repeated patterns.
Her mind is beyond
all foresight.
Her able hands do not accept
patterns or models.
Whatever comes forth, comes forth,
but she who is will make it.

The colors of her threads
are firm:
blood,
sweat,
perseverance,
tears,
struggle,
and hope.
Colors that do not fade
with time.

The children of the children
of our children
will recognize the seal
of the Old Weaver.
Maybe then
it will receive a name.

But as a model,
it can never again
be repeated.

Each morning I have seen
how her fingers
choose the threads
one by one.
Her loom makes no noise,
and men
give it no importance.

None-the-less,
the design
that emerges from her mind
hour after hour
will appear in the threads
of many colors,
in figures and symbols
which no one, ever again,
will be able to erase
or un-do.[28]

3

The Loom of Authority:
Mutuality and Solidarity

Weaving is done on a loom. The success of a design does not depend on the loom, however, but rather on the awareness, imagination, and intuition that the person who is creating possesses. . . . The loom is the weaver's most important tool. Whether it is complex or simple, one of the major functions of a loom is to keep the warp threads in order and under tension. . . . The industrial power loom, the hand loom, the tapestry loom, and the frame loom all have certain characteristics in common and follow the same fundamental weaving process. The main differences are the speed with which something is woven and the possible combinations of form, shape, yarn, thread manipulation, and organization.[1]

The nature of pastoral authority is of paramount concern in the field of homiletics. Theologians and scholars wrestling with the nature of proclamation and preachers struggling with the purpose and authenticity of their task must continually address the issue of authority. For centuries men have primarily defined the authority of the preacher from their own male experience, with little if any acknowledgment that authority might be understood and embodied differently in the lives and ministry of women preachers. The intention of this chapter is to name and to explore several distinctive insights and understandings about authority that emerge from female experience and feminist scholarship.

The Loom of Authority

What understandings of authority provide the foundation, or loom, of our preaching ministry? Continuing to develop the weaving metaphor for preaching from a feminist perspective, I want to suggest that the preacher's understanding of authority becomes the basic loom on which she or he weaves the preaching experience. The loom is the basic structure on which weaving takes place. It is foundational to the entire weaving craft. The many variations of looms provide the possibility for a variety of woven patterns and creations; nevertheless, a weaver's loom is basic to the entire creative process.

A Critique of Traditional Homiletical Thought on Authority

It is of no small coincidence that while many women preachers are articulating a different way of understanding authority, some contemporary scholars in homiletics are making every attempt to shore up traditional views. There is little difference, in the definitions and sources of the preacher's authority, between those articulated in preaching books published very recently and those found in preaching books published at least ten to twenty years ago. Preaching textbooks and resources show little awareness of the critique of feminist liberation theology upon issues such as hierarchical power, unquestioned biblical authority, and the ultimate authority of tradition. These are problematic areas for feminists, and the critique of such understandings of authority and power applies to all theological disciplines, including homiletics.

While many white male scholars are resorting to very traditional understandings of authority, they also will admit that much of traditional preaching method and theology is in need of substantial reform. There is some agreement among homileticians that the church needs new ways of understanding the preacher's authority. The automatic authority once given to the preacher is no longer present in many places. The ecclesiastical authority bestowed on the preacher from the church's hierarchical bodies means little to communities who find the content and style of Christian preaching irrelevant and often judgmental. Perhaps in the midst of this critique, which is an oft-repeated one, a different view of power, authority, and relatedness is needed.

While little has been written from a feminist perspective specifically addressing homiletical issues of authority, an evocative book that raises important questions about authority is *Feminist Interpretation of the Bible,* edited by Letty M. Russell. It provides some important insights into the transformation of authority from a feminist perspective. Barbara Brown Zikmund, in her article "Feminist Consciousness in Historical Perspective," writes of the evolution of feminist consciousness:

> As women have become more self-conscious about themselves, their relationship to authority, especially religious authority, has changed. Today, Christian and Jewish women have new understandings of their place in religious communities and their relationship to scripture. This new understanding may be called a "feminist critical consciousness."[2]

This feminist critical consciousness also applies to the craft of preaching. Women are beginning to redefine authority and the understandings of intimacy that flow from these new definitions. These new definitions of authority take into account women's experience of marginality and oppression. Religious authority is being questioned and reexamined as women take their own religious truths and insights more seriously. The traditional categories of religious authority, still claimed as primary sources of authority by the scholars who dominate the field of homiletical thought, are called into question by this rising critical consciousness.

In the same volume, Letty Russell speaks about the critical feminist consciousness in yet another way when she writes about a feminist paradigm of authority:

> The feminist paradigm of authority is a shift in interpretive framework that affects all the authority structures in religion and society, including the claim that scripture evokes our consent to faith and action. The prevailing paradigm

of authority in Christian and Jewish religion is one of authority as domination.[3]

The critical feminist consciousness spoken about within feminist theological scholarship ultimately produces a dramatic and thorough confrontation and critique of prevailing theological understandings of authority and domination. As more sources of authority are explored, particularly by feminists, sources of authority that are based on hierarchy, domination, and inequality become idolatrous and unacceptable to a growing number of women and men preachers and theologians.

I believe the way we define and exercise authority will critically determine the way we then shape and create intimacy, and vice versa. There is a fundamental interwoven connection between authority and intimacy for many women, and especially for self-conscious feminists. Many women and men are becoming increasingly aware of the blatant contradictions that exist between the language of mutuality and dialogue, and the theology and structures of domination. These contradictions surface in the theory and practice of homiletics. In the methodology section of many homiletics books is found language of creativity and dialogue as well as an attempt to critique the traditional notion of the preacher's "set-apartness." Yet in those very sources one seldom finds a critique of traditional understandings of authority or a willingness to link those sources of authority to a deep patriarchal bias.

Before delving into the specific insights of women's scholarship and its illumination of authority, a basic question of definition must be addressed. This pertains to patriarchal language and traditional structures that control meaning. I question the very term *authority* and its appropriateness for a description of women's preaching.[4]

Authority in preaching has traditionally been defined as that quality of proclamation that pertains to special rights, power, knowledge, and capacity to influence or transform. James W. Cox, in his most recent book, enumerates six sources of the preacher's authority: divine call, ordination, education, experience, integrity of character, and biblical text.[5] Even though Cox speaks about the way the preacher shares authority and affirms that that authority ultimately rests within the total community, he nevertheless refers to sources of authority that promote and encourage the preacher's separateness and special status. This listing of the sources of authority is repeated in much of the literature. Fred B. Craddock, in his book *Preaching,* describes authority in a section on preaching and the nature of the preacher: "Authority is that which gives one the right to speak. It is ecclesiastical by reason of ordination; it is charismatic by reason of a call; it is personal by reason of talent and education; it is democratic by reason of the willingness of the listeners to give their attention."[6] Even though Craddock attempts to express the nature of the preacher's authority in somewhat less dominating ways, the flavor of separateness still persists.

From a feminist perspective, these sources of the preacher's authority, as well as the very word *authority* itself, are called into question. Many women would not speak of authority as that which gives them the "right" to speak. Authority has to do with a quality of content, a mode of communication, and an authenticity of message which make the preaching craft and the moment of proclamation credible, honest, and life-transforming for speaker and listener alike. For many, preaching is not so much a matter of the right and privilege of the position with all of its distinctive power; rather it is a craft of authenticity weaving together mutuality, solidarity, and deeper faith sharing. Therefore, authority and intimacy are of necessity inextricably woven together in feminist preaching.

The criteria for effective preaching held by many male homiletics scholars and preachers appear to be persuasion and one's ability to influence the listener. The criteria for many women preachers appear to be creating or enabling a quality of faith connection and participating in the transforming power of true solidarity in community. At a time when solidarity and equality are great priorities of justice and right-relatedness, the traditional sources of authority simply are no longer appropriate. In fact, they are in contradiction to a feminist vision within the church and the world.

This is not to deny the reality of ordination, divine call, biblical text, education, and giftedness associated with the particular role of the preacher. I am suggesting that a great many women and men in ministry today find themselves struggling to redefine and name these realities of ordained ministry and preaching in new, increasingly inclusive ways. Letty Russell again sheds light on the effort to name authority in ministry and preaching with her continual work on an emerging feminist paradigm:

> The emerging feminist paradigm that tries to make sense of biblical and theological truth claims is that of authority as partnership or community. . . . Authority is exercised *in* community and not *over* community and tends to reinforce ideas of cooperation, with contributions from a wide diversity of persons enriching the whole.[7]

I hope that the church eventually will move away from the use of the word *authority* and will choose another, more liberating term to describe the dynamics involved in authentic, transforming proclamation. Traditional understandings of authority are being critiqued not only because they contribute to a theology of domination, separation, and hierarchy, but also because the traditional categories are no longer in harmony with the ways in which many women are growing to understand themselves and their world and faith perspectives.

Understanding the Loom of Women's Authority

I have already noted that many feminist women might speak of authority in relation to preaching: that is, through a quality of content, a level of mutuality in communication, and a high degree of authenticity in their message. Following my research in women's psychology, I am even more encouraged to believe that women would prefer to speak of authority not as some special right or privilege, but rather as a quality of presence, mutuality, and integrity. For feminist women, authority is not something one possesses or the way one dominates a community of people or another individual; rather it is a quality of humanness that is so persuasive and honest that it calls people into connection and solidarity.

Not only are many traditional understandings of authority oppressive because they are rooted in concepts of domination and special privilege, but they are also false definitions in the light of most women's actual experience. In the case of preaching, women's experience often has been that divine call, ordination, education, experience, and biblical text give them only limited authority in the church or society. This is in clear contrast to the authority that many males automatically attain as a result of these same ecclesiastical and cultural structures. Women have learned all too painfully that these sources often are inadequate in the actual authority of their ministry. I do not disclaim them as powerful symbols altogether, but there is no immediate correlation between these sources that grant power and the actual experience of authority in women's proclamation. We pause and ask ourselves what kind of authority women have and what kind might women wish to have, given their distinctive female worldview and psychology.

In this task of redefining authority from the perspective of female experience, I will draw on a variety of sources in women's psychology and selected work in feminist theology. The basic truth that emerges from all these sources regarding women's redefinition of authority is: Out of women's experience and feminist critique comes a distinctive way of defining power, strength, and authority not commonly understood today in a white male-dominated society. New definitions and ways of thinking about power and authority arise from within female experience and scholarship.

Dorothy E. Smith, in her contribution to the collection *The Prism of Sex*, describes and builds a distinctive sociology for women. Women are still new to the task of fully and courageously speaking their truths and their world perspectives. Smith offers the struggle of women poets to speak from their own center as a vision to all women seeking to claim the power of female experiences:

> A poetry that is linked to experience through the active participation of the poet herself. A poetry that is real, because the voice that speaks it is as real as the poet can be about herself. A poetry that is revolutionary, because by expressing the vision of real women it challenges the patriarchal premises of society itself.[8]

This vision of authenticity and power is a radically different view of authority. Its presence as a new kind of women's power signals deep integrity between what is articulated and the real-life experience of the poet. It also creates a solidarity with those who hear such an authentic and honest voice. It is a kind of power that is created out of risk and mutuality, not an authority of position, role, or status. It is an authority of radical selfhood, radical realness, and radical oneness *with* the hearer. Ultimately, it is a kind of power that is rooted in women's distinctive female wisdom and experience and women's particular subjectivities.[9] It is a power that assumes that all of life is subjective, and that when people push the depths of their own human experience they have the potential to link in solidarity with others.

There are other ways power and authority are spoken about and defined by women. In defining authority anew, women make strong connections between the ways they perceive and experience relatedness and intimacy, and the ways they express integrity and create solidarity. Authority, perhaps better understood as integrity and ultimate solidarity, is created and experienced in direct relation to the quality of connection and intimacy that humans experience with each other in communication and interaction. Women are "more likely than men to believe that, ideally, all activity should lead to an increased emotional connection with others."[10] The mark of authenticity and women's authority is deep connection to one's self, to God, and to others. Isabel Carter Heyward, in *The Redemption of God,* speaks clearly and powerfully about differences in authority when she seeks to "re-image" Jesus and the kind of authority he ultimately possessed and lived:

> Authority *(exousia)* is power that has been granted, power that is socially licensed or allowed. A person with *exousia* has been granted the right to power. . . .
>
> Re-image a Jesus whose "authority" was not *exousia,* but rather *dunamis:* raw power, self-attributed, socially illegitimate; a Jesus who was granted authority by that which he knew to be God on the basis of his realization of

his power *(dunamis);* a Jesus whose authority among
human beings was unmediated and unlicensed. . . .

Re-image our own humanity, in which our relation to
God is the wellspring of our movement into and through
ambiguity and tension toward an emerging sense of what
it means to be human: to have *dunamis,* to relate, to claim
exousia. [11]

This is in stark contrast to traditional ways of understanding
authority as a quality of "set-apartness" and separation. Intimacy and authenticity work together. Authenticity helps enable
the connections to be made between people, and intimacy
evokes and demands authenticity. When intimacy and authority
work together and are a part of an interwoven whole, then the
words and living actions of a person have power and credibility.
Power and authority traditionally defined have almost always
meant power *for* oneself and power *over* others.[12] Power has
seldom been defined in terms of mutual power and exchange,
solidarity, and human connection at all levels of experience.
Power and authority have not yet been transformed by the
special values women can bring to these qualities in life. Yet
slowly, the definitions are expanding to take into account
women's distinctive perspective.

Ann Belford Ulanov, in her book *Receiving Woman,* focuses
an entire chapter on the phenomenon of women and authority.
She encourages and challenges women to face the issues of their
own authority and to claim its distinctive quality. "We live now
in a historical era of unparalleled opportunities for fundamental
changes of consciousness. There are accessible to us in increasingly articulated form the images, concepts, and symbols of the
feminine modality of being. . . . Women who would receive all
of themselves and who insist on being received by others as all
of themselves, lead the way at the moment in shaping what
could become a radically new consciousness."[13] For women to
know and realize the full power of their new definitions, seeing
the male as normative must be exposed as the oppressive illusion
that it is, and total relational transformation must be embraced.

Ulanov ultimately affirms three important elements pertaining to women's distinctive authority: (1) the capacity to stand firm as women on what we say and know; (2) the commitment women have to mutuality and to nonhierarchical ways of communicating and relating; and (3) the conviction that the illumination of our own personal experience as women is intimately and fundamentally connected to all of collective human experience; thus we claim our distinctiveness in order to increase the strength and solidarity of the entire human community.[14]

When Ulanov speaks about our ability to stand firmly behind what we say and what we know, she addresses the same power I earlier identified in relation to the power of the contemporary woman poet. Women must believe their own female experience before they can fully believe their own voices. They must believe what they say and its wisdom for the human community before they will be able to stand firmly behind their own articulations. They must believe what they know even when it is disputed, disregarded, or despised. The capacity to stand firmly behind what we say and what we know is an important aspect of women's power and authenticity.

When Ulanov speaks about women's basic underlying commitment to mutuality and nonhierarchical relating, she affirms a truth that opposes all traditional understandings of authority: that authority and authenticity are not inseparably linked to domination and subordination. In fact, oppressive power of any kind destroys the possibility for true authenticity and integrity of human interaction. Authority by this new definition, then, becomes a collective quality of connection and sharing, an experience of solidarity where insights and views are expressed for the empowerment of all.

Authority from a woman's perspective is much more a meeting of truths and a mutual exchange of perspectives for the good of all than it is the capacity to influence, control, or dominate. Linked with feminist understandings of nonhierarchical ways of relating and sharing truths is the final point Ulanov explores—the belief that women's experience is needed by our world in order to heal and transform patterns of oppression and subordination. This aspect of women's power and commitment to solidarity relates to the world's need for a new visionary perspective and worldview concerning mutuality and wholeness.

One might see this as presumptuous. However, men have assumed since the beginning of time that the world needed their distinct perspective, and they then systematically structured that worldview into all the structures of cultural reality. It is time for women to realize that our perspective is sorely needed as a worldview that has never been given full acknowledgment or appreciation for its own distinctive power and potential goodness. Where I may stand in conflict with Ulanov's basic contention centers around the "price or cost" of being a healing agent. If this implies that women will one more time fail to confront, challenge, and critique experiences and structures of oppression, then I am in direct opposition. If healing assumes struggle and confrontation on the way to wholistic relatedness and healing, I am in support.

Women's authority and authenticity are seldom welcomed by mainline society and the dominant culture. Women must claim the right to own their own authority and must understand that being truly authentic persons in a patriarchal culture will be risky indeed. Women must realize that "in our time we have heard a great deal about people's lack of authenticity. What we cannot hear so clearly is that, for half of the population, the attempt at authenticity requires a clear and direct risk."[15]

For women, power, authority, or authenticity demands of us a commitment to self-determination. This does not arise from individualism or self-enhancement primarily, but rises from a growing awareness that the power and credibility of our women's experience have been systematically denied us and the larger human community, and this must cease. "Having the opportunity to talk about one's life, to give an account of it, to interpret it, is integral to leading that life rather than being led through it. . . . Part of human life, human living, is talking about it, and we [women] can be sure that being silenced in one's own account of one's life is a kind of amputation that signals oppression."[16] Not only has there been an amputation of individual voices from individual women, but the collective experiences and wisdom of women have been denied to the total human community. A collective commitment on the part of women to voice their life realities and truths about intimacy and authority is absolutely essential if we are to redefine integrity, mutuality, and human solidarity from the particular and distinctive voice of female experience.

In *Daughters of Copper Woman,* by Anne Cameron, a book about the native people of Vancouver Island, basic female experience is explored and celebrated as ancient human wisdom and authority. In one story, Copper Woman, who is the protector of the secrets of female wisdom, is ready to die. It is her task to pass on this wisdom before she returns to the earth and sky. After speaking of this treasured wisdom to her daughter, Hai Nai Yu, she walks to the beach, becomes a spirit, and turns her bones into a broom and a loom. This is a powerful image! With her very being Copper Woman forms the loom from which she weaves destiny and reality, and the spirit that permeates the loom is a part of all creation. Copper Woman reminds us that the loom of our transforming, creative power, the loom of our life and faith weaving, is our woman's wisdom—a large source of our authority.[17]

As we seek to articulate and understand the distinctive quality of women and their preaching, this loom is where we must begin. The kind of loom we are determines the very nature of our weaving. In terms of authority, women's scholarship and its illumination of female experience suggest that many women begin with a loom named mutuality and solidarity. Preaching from a feminist perspective roots authority in mutuality and solidarity in the faith community.

Mutuality and solidarity are clearly nonauthoritarian, non-hierarchical qualities of human relatedness and interaction. In mutuality, people possess or hold something in common. In solidarity, people experience oneness in nature, relations, interest, or vision. Both qualities of human connection imply the sharing of power, the honoring of truths, and the celebration of the web of interdependence. These qualities point to the transformation of traditional ways of understanding the proclamation of faith and mystery.

John Killinger says, "The preacher of the gospel is not doing something new, however original he or she may feel."[18] I heartily disagree with his assertion. I believe that women are doing something radically new and different in their preaching, and pastors and scholars alike are struggling to name this difference more clearly. For women, their distinctive preaching authority is not a matter of being "original" in their insights, biblical interpretations, or creative styles of delivery, although all of these dimensions to preaching are important. Women's authority is rooted in the very act of naming and speaking words of faith and hope from the perspective of being female.

This perspective has never been fully voiced before in the history of the church or world. This kind of authority has little to do with outside structures, or rights, or privileges; rather it has to do with a quality of naming and witnessing that is born from within the lives and souls of faithful women. This naming has to do with celebrating the web of human relatedness and creating solidarity. Even to suggest that there exists this kind of authority is a powerful and distinctively female assertion. One might object to this definition of the locus of women's authority as being overly subjective and personal. For women to claim their own authority, however, is not to dismiss the authority of the experience of another, but rather to be clear about one's own authority of experience. Nelle Morton, in *The Journey Is Home,* speaks about the importance of individuals' and groups' claiming their own voices, and the integrity of not assuming that one's voice speaks for the whole:

> Thus it is customary to label women's theological work as "feminist theology" while maintaining the mainstream theological work as "theology," . . . or to dismiss the rising new spirituality among women as vaporous, shallow nature worship, while maintaining the traditional nomenclature as the true spiritual in spite of its domestication and control. It is not wrong to be partial. The wrongness comes when the partial parades as the whole.[19]

For too long the partial has paraded as the whole. White male preachers and homileticians have assumed that their perceptions and insights into preaching were shared by the whole. Women are beginning to challenge this assumption and are learning how to claim the sources of their own authority.

Because many women understand authority in distinctive ways, both the content and the process of proclamation are transformed. I will elaborate much more fully on the content of

women's preaching in chapters 4 and 5 as I seek to weave
women's understanding of authority with their equally strong
commitments to feminist liberation theology as critique and
vision for the Christian tradition. I summarize here some final
insights about the process of women's preaching, shaped by a
loom of mutuality and solidarity.

Preaching from a feminist perspective involves solidarity and
oneness, not elite detachment and individual power. It is not
talking about solidarity; it is about creating it by the very act of
proclamation. Preaching from a feminist perspective asserts that
greatest mutuality is achieved and experienced among equals.
Thus, in preaching, the truths of the entire community need to
be honored, expressed, and sought out if true mutuality is at the
heart of faith sharing. Elisabeth Schüssler Fiorenza confronts us
with the demands of mutuality and solidarity:

> The impoverishment of preaching today is not due to the
> lack of able preachers, but due to a structural clericalism
> with demands that one single group of Christians—the
> ordained—articulate the richness and fullness of all Chris-
> tians' God-experiences today.[20]

Because women themselves have been excluded from the act of
preaching for centuries, we know that no one person or group
of people can dominate this act of faith if true solidarity in
community is ever to come to pass. Preaching from a feminist
perspective must involve an increasing commitment to open to
all people the opportunity for proclaiming faith truths and to
work toward integrating the voices of all silenced people into the
content and truths of our words. The process of ever-expanding
inclusiveness is at the center of solidarity.

Our true understandings and biases can be revealed in many
ways. John Killinger, for example, suggests that one might ask
oneself three questions prior to constructing a sermon. These
questions demonstrate in subtle but clear ways an authoritarian,
yet often undisputed, approach to the craft. The questions are
these: "What am I trying to do to these people? What do I wish
them to see? What would I like to have happen in their minds
as I preach?"[21]

The implications underlying these questions reflect a process of preaching that supports the dichotomy of preacher and community as separate and distinct realities. The questions would be very different if they were designed to help a preacher construct a sermon event or a moment of proclamation that was rooted in solidarity. They might then read: In this moment of faith sharing, what are we trying to explore, create, or articulate together? What can we all see together in these moments of proclamation? What do you illumine for me in terms of mystery and faith, what do I illumine for you, and what truths can we bring to light together? What are our hopes as a community for these shared moments together? What do we hope will happen?

These very different guiding questions, if used to shape our preaching, will root the process of proclamation much more deeply in creating mutuality and solidarity. When one understands the goal of preaching to be the creation of solidarity, one must trust each person in the community to do her or his own searching, struggling, celebrating, and naming.

Fred Craddock, in *Overhearing the Gospel,* speaks about a style of indirect preaching that allows for people to hear their own truths. "To deliver a message for overhearing, the speaker will need to trust fully in the message to create its own effect, trust the listener to exercise his freedom responsibly, and trust the process, however fragile and accidental it may appear, to be powerful."[22] This preaching process does not tell people what to believe, nor does it assume the preacher has truths that all people should possess. It assumes, on the other hand, that people have the power to discover their own truths and faith, and affirms that this process of discovery is enhanced and made richer in community. This indirect overhearing process is much more in harmony with the attempts of women to create solidarity and mutuality.

Women believe in solidarity not only because it is rooted in the concept of relatedness and intimacy—those aspects of life that appear to be in harmony with much of female experience and development—but because they know solidarity to be a matter of justice as well. All marginalized people know what it means to have their voices silenced and ignored. We are all too familiar with the luxury of individual voices at the expense of community expression and truth. It is hoped that this is a pattern that women, and growing numbers of men, will resist, knowing in a profound way that it only leads to the oppression of those who have no power and privilege. Voicing truth is always a matter of justice.

Finally, new understandings of authority are rooted in a belief that preaching is the sharing of everyday human struggles and experiences rather than the articulating of elite and specialized truth. Mutuality and solidarity depend on the equal worth of all, not the superior valuing of a few. Mutuality and solidarity prize the gifts and insights of all. Alice Walker, in a poem entitled "We Alone," names this quality of solidarity that appreciates the giftedness of all truths and all people, and challenges us to make this act of honoring all people central to our life and work:

> We alone can devalue gold
> by not caring
> if it falls or rises
> in the marketplace.
> Wherever there is gold
> there is a chain, you know,
> and if your chain is gold
> so much the worse
> for you.
> Feathers, shells,
> and sea-shaped stones
> are all as rare.
> This could be our revolution:
> To love what is plentiful
> as much as
> what's scarce.[23]

4

The Warp of Critique: New Theological Naming

Preparing the loom for action consists in winding the warp, beaming it; and threading it. These processes are called "Setting up the Loom" by some weavers and "Dressing the Loom" by others. Both terms are appropriate, for a loom that is properly threaded for use has attractive rows of warp threads stretched to an even tension, like so many violin strings. When these are arranged in perfect order, running parallel through the reed and glistening in their fibrous sheen, the loom is indeed "set up" or "dressed" for the occasion of starting to weave. The more perfect the warp, the better the weaving will be. A poor warp produces imperfect cloth throughout its entire length. The dressing process may be regarded as a preparatory period full of anticipation for future work.[1]

The critique we feminists make of Christianity involves a long agenda for theological change. It requires an extended and profound rethinking of all the language, images, and metaphors central to Christian theology, a re-visioning that will surely not be exhausted soon.[2]

Standing within the Christian tradition there are several major strands of transforming critique that many feminist preachers are stretching onto the loom of their preaching. Each of these strands is critical for preaching and exerts powerful influence on the transformation of the preaching craft. The new theological naming that Christian feminist preachers weave into their proclamations involves a critique of traditional God language, Christology, and biblical hermeneutics. These new threads of theological naming become the basic warp threads for weaving. When I speak of new theological naming, I am referring to the disciplined, transforming work of Christian feminist theologians, ethicists, biblical scholars, historians, and women in pastoral ministry. I am speaking about work that attempts to wage a thorough and systematic critique of every aspect of the Christian tradition. Feminist theology begins with women's experience of marginalization and then seeks to weave that experience through theological categories, ethical paradigms, biblical hermeneutics, the reconstruction of church history, and the practice of Christian ministry.

Feminist theologians make the assumption that patriarchal values permeate the Christian tradition and that an androcentric worldview undergirds it in its present form. Feminists vary greatly as to the severity of their critique, but all operate out of a basic understanding that the tradition stands in need of liberating transformation. Feminist theology is part of the larger feminist movement seeking many levels of social and ecclesiastical change. Elisabeth Schüssler Fiorenza, in *Bread Not Stone,* describes the breadth and depth of feminist theological critique in these words:

> Feminist theologies introduce a radical shift into all forms of traditional theology, for they insist that the central commitment and accountability for feminist theologians is not to *the* church as a male institution but to women in the churches, not to *the* tradition as such but to a feminist transformation of Christian traditions, not to *the* Bible as a whole but to the liberating Word of God finding expression in the biblical writings.[3]

It is this critical aspect of feminist liberation theology that is addressed in this chapter. I will explore several strands of feminist critique concerning God language, Christology, and biblical hermeneutics. Feminist theologians, ethicists, biblical scholars, and historians have been naming and developing these strands of critique for several years. It is women and men serving in local church ministry, campus ministry settings, denominational structures and systems, however, who bear the major burden of discerning how to translate much of this scholarship to diverse and often conservative local communities. The feminist Christian woman or man who has the daily and weekly responsibility of preaching in a local context must struggle with the issues of God language, Christology, and biblical interpretation in the practice of her or his ministry and acts of proclamation. This is a difficult and often isolating task.

For Christian feminists who are also preachers, the task of proclamation is demanding and painful at many levels, three of which are particularly crucial.

First, the preacher is often the sole person in a local community giving expression to any kind of feminist critique of the tradition. In this situation of isolation one experiences pressure to compromise one's voice and theology.

Second, the skills needed to engage in feminist theological work with integrity are many. Preaching with a feminist consciousness calls for skills in feminist theology, feminist biblical hermeneutics, and feminist historical reconstruction, in addition to an awareness of the larger sociopolitical reality in which patriarchal Christianity rests.

Third, the task of preaching is further complicated for many Christian feminists by a deep ambiguity about the tradition itself and our position within it. The number of women in Christian ministry who struggle daily with their own relationship to Christianity is not to be underestimated, and there are a growing number of men who also struggle. This ambiguity is not to be mistaken for a lack of clarity about one's call to ministry or even one's call and desire to preach. Preaching is difficult at best; and for Christian feminists who attempt to be responsive to critical feminist theological scholarship and to the spiritual and pastoral needs of a community, it is an even more complex and challenging liberation act.

There is a simple yet profound Navajo story that has spoken much truth to me about my own struggle/journey with the Christian tradition and my ongoing attempts to integrate various aspects of it into my religious life. Miska Miles's *Annie and the Old One* speaks about the painful realities we must weave into our lives, and the wisdom and new visions that come from that weaving. Annie's grandmother will "return to Mother Earth" when the new rug is taken from the loom. As Annie's mother continues to weave the new rug to sell at the market-place for food and needed goods, Annie plots in her mind and heart how to prevent the rug from being completed. She gets into trouble at school in the hope that her parents will come to school and there will be one day her mother will not weave. She lets the sheep out of their pen in the hope that there will be one day her mother will not weave. For several nights, hoping to prolong the inevitable, Annie slips to the loom and removes strands of wool. One night her grandmother touches her shoul-der while she is at the loom removing strands, and sends her gently back to bed. The next day the two of them walk and talk, sharing many things:

> Grandmother says, "My granddaughter, you have tried to hold back time. This cannot be done. The sun comes up from the edge of earth in the morning. It returns to the edge of earth in the evening. Earth, from which good things come for the living creatures on it. Earth, to which all creatures finally go." Annie understood many things as they talked. She knew that she was a part of the earth and the things on it. She would always be a part of the earth, just as her grandmother had always been, just as her grand-mother would always be, always and forever. And Annie was breathless with the wonder of it.[4]

After their talk, Annie and her grandmother walked back to the hogan. Annie picked up the weaving stick that her grandmother had given her, she picked up a strand of gray wool, and she started to weave.

There are strands of life, strands of reality, that are very painful to weave into our tapestries of life. We may refuse to weave the strands into our lives, but the strands do not disap-pear, the realities do not cease to be present in our world. For me and for many Christian feminists, I encounter the Christian tradition with the same kind of avoidance, resistance, sadness, and anger that Annie encountered in her grandmother's im-pending death. The tradition does not disappear, nor does the reality of it cease to claim my loyalty and commitment. It is my heritage and my story, and thus far my efforts are toward integration rather than departure. Beverly Harrison, in "The Power of Anger in the Work of Love," says, "If only the *withholding* of power were adequate to bring about social change in our world, undoing oppression would not be difficult. However, we women should be the last to allow ourselves to be trapped in a 'spiritualizing' notion that real change in our flesh and blood world ever comes from absenting ourselves from what is going on in that world."[5]

Even though many women at times fantasize about leaving the Christian tradition, many of us also know that to absent ourselves from it is to leave it unchanged. We remain out of a commitment to liberation for women in particular and a conviction to structural change for justice in behalf of all.

Basic Warp Threads

When preaching from a feminist perspective, the warp threads in a weaving are the particular threads of the Christian tradition that must be claimed, critiqued, and understood as foundational concerns and issues within the homiletical task. When one initially undertakes to weave, one must decide the width and the length of the warp, the texture of it, and the color patterns. The size, texture, and color of the basic warp threads will determine much of the nature of the entire weaving.

All Loom Weaving Begins with the Warp

In preaching from a feminist perspective, crucial decisions must be made about the foundational warp threads of preaching that undergird the entire proclamation weaving. Some of the questions that surface as women and men seek to choose the warp threads of their preaching are these: What theology will undergird my preaching? Where do I stand in relation to images and language for God? How do I understand the historical Jesus and the faith affirmation of the Christ? What kind of authority do I give scripture, and what criteria will I use in my own biblical hermeneutics?

Even though there are diverse decisions that Christian feminists will make concerning these questions, there is a prophetic edge to all preaching from a feminist perspective. I pose here an alternative definition for *prophetic* to the one commonly understood in homiletics literature and in Christian biblical theology in general. Often a prophet is seen as a lone individual bearing a difficult and confronting word of truth to a community. Even though the prophet stands within the community of faith, he or she is also "set apart." This model of prophet not only is inadequate but also is inconsistent with a feminist worldview. For those who preach from a feminist perspective, one views prophetic words and messages as they arise out of collective experience and wisdom. In the specific case of the feminist critique of the Christian tradition, there are clearly collective voices of prophetic insight and critical vision spoken by an entire movement of individuals and communities. The foundational threads of our weaving, our warp threads for preaching, are fundamentally different from the warp threads of most male and female preachers who are not rooted in feminist theology.

Homiletics literature and the actual preaching content of many men and women reflect little substantial critique of the Christian tradition. Traditional modes of biblical interpretation and theological reflection are still affirmed as normative and inclusive of all human experience and faith. By contrast, Christian feminists engaged in the craft and task of preaching bring a prophetic quality to their proclamation at several levels: (1) Critical feminist theology seeks to critique the Christian tradition in such a way that it becomes responsive and relevant to the particularities of all human experience. One strand of human experience must never represent or speak for another. (2) The critique Christian feminists offer in relation to God language, Christology, and biblical hermeneutics becomes one of our most prophetic voices in preaching. This relentless critique becomes a faithful and prophetic voice we can offer on behalf of a God who calls the human community into liberation and out of oppressive, dehumanizing structures. (3) In terms of the specific content of women's preaching, there exists the possibility for a *distinctive* prophetic quality as well. Justo and Catherine Gonzalez best express this possibility in their book *Liberation Preaching:*

> If the major portion of the Bible is written by those who, in their own social situation, are the powerless and oppressed, if it is their perspective on the activity of God that is given us by Scripture, then surely a more accurate interpretation of the biblical word can be gained by those who currently stand in a parallel place in our own societies than by those who are powerful.[6]

All who preach from a feminist perspective must strip away years of patriarchal interpretations and a pervasive androcentric worldview within the biblical narratives themselves in order to recover the voice of the powerless and oppressed. For women, when a point of identification is made between our own women's marginalization and the oppression of those in the stories of scripture, this point of intersection becomes a rich source of possibilities for liberating and faithful preaching. Men are challenged to find their own marginalized experiences as points of connection.

Choosing the particular feminist warp threads of God language, Christology, and biblical hermeneutics becomes a prophetic and transforming critique of preaching. Ultimately what this means is that Christian feminists, whose preaching is self-consciously informed by critical feminist theological thought, begin the weaving/preaching act with warp strands entirely different from those of preachers who begin their task giving unquestioned authority to the Christian tradition as it presently stands.

A more traditional way of viewing the whole issue of the warp strands of preaching is to locate the discussion in the context of an analysis of proclamation which affirms that preaching is an act of theologizing:

> Preaching is the final expression of theology. It has been toward preaching that theology has been tending. . . . If the desired integration is to take place in theology, it may begin with the recognition of the legitimacy of preaching as a theological discipline.[7]

As many women preach, their preaching is not just an expression of theology; it is a particular expression of feminist liberation theology. Let me illuminate more clearly and fully what some of those new warp threads look like in the new naming of traditional God language, Christology, and biblical hermeneutics.

God Language

In the context of preaching, God language pertains to how we fundamentally understand and image the God about whom we preach, the specific language we use to describe human/God relationships, and how we view the nature of sacred reality in our lives. The way many feminist Christian preachers understand God and the inclusive ways they desire to talk about God often become the first major theological struggle in the craft and act of preaching. This struggle remains alive, constant, and poignant for many women and men who preach regularly in communities of faith. To understand the issue more completely and to name the myriad resources feminist preachers are drawing from in order to reweave their God language and understandings, I will summarize portions of feminist theological thought that shape and influence many women preachers. This scholarship increasingly is claiming the attention and commitment of many men as well. Being a woman who has been preaching regularly for over ten years, I will use my own theological evolution as illustrative example of the journeys of many white, middle-class, Protestant women and men in ministry.

Mary Daly's classic book *Beyond God the Father: Toward a Philosophy of Women's Liberation,* published in 1973, was my first exposure to a radical critique of traditional patriarchal Christianity. She specifically confronts the destructive nature of traditional God language and offers some constructive suggestions about ways the church might liberate its God images and understandings. Her ultimate belief is in the power of women to name the reality of God in new and transforming ways. Many of us began reading her stinging critique and found that our theology and our images were changing as a result:

> Three false deities still haunt the prayers, hymns, sermons, and religious education of Christianity. . . . One of the false

deities to be dethroned is the God of explanation. . . . Another idol is the God of otherworldliness . . . [and the] third idol . . . is the God who is the Judge of "sin," who confirms the rightness of rules and roles of the reigning system, maintaining false consciences and self-destructive guilt feelings.[8]

Daly goes on to point out how these images and theologies of God have been used specifically to reinforce women's oppression. The God of explanation confirms that women's present roles and experiences of oppression are "God's will"; the God of otherworldliness encourages women to deny their own power now in hopes of some future heavenly reward; and the God of judgment totally reinforces the system of patriarchal domination while condemning anyone who challenges present power structures and systems.

Daly begins to claim for all of us as women the power and right to name God out of our own female experience:

The unfolding of God, then, is an event in which women participate as we participate in our own revolution. . . . Women have had the power of *naming* stolen from us. We have not been free to use our own power to name ourselves, the world, or God.[9]

Daly's book has had tremendous influence on the shaping of many Christian feminists' understandings of God. Of most importance, it was one of the first theological resources for many of us that encouraged women to claim the freedom to begin to name God for ourselves and in community with other women. Much of feminist scholarship today is indebted to the courageous thought of Mary Daly's early work.

The early stages of my own struggle with God language and imagery were largely reactive. I had never related deeply to images of God as father; thus Daly's work served to reaffirm for me a basic lack of identification with male God language. I had always felt this tension but knew no words to express it. In my early years of preaching I knew that I did not want to use exclusive father God imagery and language, but I was at a great loss to image and name God anew. It was at this point in my own journey and in the evolution of the feminist movement within the Christian church that women, and some men, began to research and reclaim images of God in the scriptures that clearly related to women's experience and faith. The resistance to changing God language is deep and strong, for this body of research did not emerge in a substantial way for several years after Daly's *Beyond God the Father.* If my own experience as a woman preacher during those years is at all typical of the experience of other women preachers, I would contend that much of the work that was happening then concerning inclusive God language was happening at a grass roots level. I had stopped using God-the-father language and started using language that was far less anthropomorphic in nature. God as creator, spirit, and sustaining presence became the new God language for me. During those years I had little knowledge of the rich biblical resources I now know exist in my own heritage.

Inclusive Biblical Images of God

In recent years there has been significant scholarship dedicated to the uncovering and reclaiming of the diversity of God language and imagery within scripture. This particular approach assumes that a much more inclusive understanding and experience of God actually can be drawn from the scriptures themselves. The Christian tradition has within its biblical roots the reality of God language that reflects more fully the female experience. Feminist theologians who begin their work with this assumption and belief assume that the starting point for our theologizing about God, and our naming of God, is with the biblical tradition. The study and exploration of specific texts yields a rich variety of images and understandings of divine presence.

One such scholar is Virginia Ramey Mollenkott. In her book *The Divine Feminine,* she attempts to show us that images of God in the scriptures do in fact reflect women's experience and activity in the world.[10] Women give birth, they bake bread, they are midwives, and they care for and empower their young. Her work is an important contribution toward our process of liberating God language and imagery, and women's self-naming.

What should not escape us in Mollenkott's theology is that it blossoms out of her understanding of *what many women do*. Many women give birth. Many women are close companions. We may be as alert or as angry as a Mother Bear; as uplifting or as sheltering as a Mother Eagle. God rises in these pages, a full-bodied female, reflecting for us the meaning of the daily lives of female-species beings.[11]

For many women and men in local communities where they are preaching, these images of God from biblical texts become a powerful way to expose people to ways of seeing and experiencing God differently. The integration of God images rooted in female experience and the movement away from exclusive father God images become for many women and men the initial warp threads of their preaching tapestry.

Even though Mollenkott and other feminist scholars give us invaluable resources for our naming of God, I want to voice a critique of this approach. Claiming and celebrating female images of God in the scriptures is an attempt to balance the predominantly androcentric and hierarchical images of God that abound in our biblical tradition. However, this critique is sometimes lacking in its clear confrontation of the biblical text for its blatant patriarchal biases and misogynist attitudes. What Mollenkott attempts to do is a kind of biblical reconstructive work in relation to God language. It is not adequate, however, to pretend that the Christian biblical tradition is fundamentally nonsexist or nonoppressive simply because there are in fact inclusive images of God sprinkled throughout the text.

Another important question concerning this approach toward the liberating of God language has to do with the diversity of female experience and the breadth of feminist concerns. Even though the images of God as midwife, mother giving birth, mother hen, female wisdom, and companion of women appear at first sight to be inclusive in relation to predominantly male God imagery, these images must be critically viewed in terms of racism, classism, heterosexism, militarism, and the breadth of female experience. A large number of these images center around birthing experiences, and there are a growing number of women who will never be biological mothers. How do women of color view these images? What is missing in the images for poor women, for women who are differently abled? Many preachers within the larger community of Christian feminists use these diverse biblical images of God without pausing to ask even deeper, more inclusive questions about the adequacy and relevance of these images.

Liberating Biblical Paradigms for God

Another approach to God language and our Christian biblical tradition is embodied in *Sexism and God-Talk* by Rosemary Radford Ruether. Rather than seek specific female images for God in the scriptures and in particular texts, she approaches the naming of God in liberating, nonhierarchical images and under-standings, under four headings.

The Prophetic God. Yahweh is known as a God who liberated the people from bondage, a God of the oppressed, and a God of those who are marginalized. "Although the predominantly male images and roles of God make Yahwism an agent in the sacralization of patriarchy, there are critical elements in Biblical theology that contradict this view of God." She goes on to say, "Yahweh is unique as the God of a tribal confederation that identifies itself as liberated slaves." This God who is a God of liberated slaves is a God who ultimately is the champion of social victims and a severe critic of the status quo, including class hierarchy.

In the New Testament, the image of the prophetic God con-tinues. Whereas liberation seemed to apply to a given commu-nity of people in the witness of the Hebrew scriptures, liberation applies to all humanity in the New Testament accounts. God now identifies with oppressed classes, ethnic groups, and women. "The New Testament contains a renewal and radicali-zation of prophetic consciousness, now applied to marginalized groups in a universal, nontribal context. . . . Class, ethnicity, and gender are now specifically singled out as the divisions overcome by redemption."[12]

The Liberating Sovereign. "Divine sovereignty and father-hood are used to break the ties of bondage under human kings and fathers. . . . The God of Exodus establishes a relationship with the people that breaks their ties with the ruling overlords." Ruether asserts that Jesus also continued the tradition established in the Hebrew scriptures of imaging and seeing God as liberating sovereign, one who is in absolute covenantal relationship with those created. Human beings are able to establish a relationship of communion and companionship with God. Jesus himself referred to God in much more personal ways than was typical of his time. "The early Jesus movement characteristically uses this concept of God as Abba to liberate the community from human dominance-dependence relationships based on kinship ties or master-servant relationships." Jesus' reference to God as Abba referred to a relationship of tenderness and care, one built on mutuality and love. Too often this radical aspect of Jesus' naming of God as divine sovereign is lost, and the concept of a community based on equality, calling for mutual service, is still undermined by a more hierarchical interpretation of sovereign. The image of liberating sovereign throughout Christian history has become distorted by images of domination. "Once the new community becomes a part of the dominant society, God as father and king can be assimilated back into the traditional patriarchal relationships and used to sacralize the authority of human lordship and patriarchy." The image of divine sovereign too easily becomes aligned with structures and systems of patriarchal domination, even though its original meaning was one of liberating presence and power.[13]

The Proscription of Idolatry. All God language, all God images, are limited and inadequate. Any attempt to capture God in language, image, or symbol is idolatrous. This fundamental theological and faith truth has been a central message in our biblical tradition. There is an underlying understanding in the biblical message that God can never be named or understood completely. "Israel is to make no picture or graven image of God; no pictorial or verbal representation of God can be taken literally. . . . The proscription of idolatry must also be extended to verbal pictures. When the word *Father* is taken literally to mean that God is male and not female, represented by males and not females, then this word becomes idolatrous." Feminist Christian women and all who preach have a strong biblical heritage to support them when they persistently confront any image of God and all language for God that has become idolatrous and representative of only partial aspects of the human community.[14]

Equivalent Images for God as Male and Female. There are equivalent images of God that include both male and female metaphors within the biblical tradition. In this section of Ruether's work on God language, she affirms and reclaims many of the same images Mollenkott addresses. Where there is sower there is woman baker; where there is shepherd, a woman with a lost coin. These metaphors and their power have often been overlooked and their real radicality ignored. "The images of male and female in these parables are equivalent. [They are drawn] from the activities of Galilean peasants. . . . The women are never described as related to or dependent on men [and] the parallel male and female images do not picture divine action in parental terms."[15]

Ruether, in describing and exploring various strands of our biblical tradition that lend themselves to more inclusive God language and imagery, attempts to reconstruct silenced parts of our tradition and celebrate more fully liberating possibilities. She finally cautions that we must question the overall adequacy of any parent image of God. I have been of this conviction for a very long time. These parental images may initially imply nurture and intimacy, but they are another kind of hierarchy, leaving human beings in permanent parent-child relationships instead of mutual relatedness and solidarity with God.[16] Ruether also would be the first to suggest the limitations of these four aspects of biblical tradition. Her thorough historical analysis of the evolution of male monotheism and patriarchal Christianity reminds us that the phenomenon of imaging God in exclusive male gender reality is not typical, but is distinctive in world religious history. "Male monotheism has been so taken for granted in Judeo-Christian culture that the peculiarity of imaging God solely through one gender has not been recognized. But such an image indicates a sharp departure from all previous human consciousness."[17] Even liberating dimensions in our biblical heritage that broaden images of God and God language always must be viewed in light of the fact that patriarchal Christianity has been eternally supported by the dominant concept of male monotheism. This concept still prevails throughout the Christian faith. Ruether simply points us to places within the tradition that may serve as sources for moving us beyond oppressive limitations in our understandings and perceptions of God.

As I spoke a word of critique about reclaiming female images for God as embodied by Mollenkott's work, I want to speak a critical word about the kind of overarching liberating paradigms that Ruether suggests. This critique is primarily in relation to her categories of prophetic God and liberating sovereign. My critique has been fundamentally informed by the work of Carol Christ in "Feminist Liberation Theology and Yahweh as Holy Warrior: An Analysis of Symbol." In this article she wages a scathing critique of feminist theology that affirms that at the heart of the biblical tradition there is a liberating message to be found, i.e., a God of liberation, a prophetic confrontation with injustice, and a historical Jesus who identifies with those who are marginal. Her critique focuses on the Hebrew Bible because this is her field of greater study. She also sets her comments in the context of a great deal of discomfort, "not wanting to perpetuate Christian anti-Judaism in a post-Christian guise." This is a discomfort Christian feminists must take seriously.

> The image of Yahweh as warrior in Exodus and the Prophets needs to be examined more directly than it has been to date by feminist theologians. It is true that the Exodus tradition of liberation from oppression and the prophetic call for social justice have inspired social liberation movements. . . . Nevertheless, I . . . cannot find these traditions adequate expressions of my spiritual-social vision.[18]

Christ then goes on to critique the God of Exodus and the prophets as a warrior God. The God who leads people out of bondage cannot be separated in Hebrew scripture from a God

who is a warrior, one who dispossesses other people from their
lands in order to make a homeland for the oppressed Israelites.
Yahweh is portrayed throughout the book of Exodus as a God
of military victory, a triumphant God who liberates one group
of people and defeats another. For Christ the contradiction is
blasphemous. Christ then moves from a critique of warrior God
to a critique of a prophetic God known to us best in the words
of the prophets. In the prophets, Yahweh is known as a punish-
ing God, a God who punishes and destroys people when they
do not act justly. The warlike images of God still abound; and
this time they are also coupled with images of an intolerant God,
a God who suppresses and annihilates all other forms of religious expression. "This vision of social justice, however, is also
embedded in the tradition of Yahweh war that was present in
Exodus; further, it is intertwined with a tradition of religious
intolerance that has been the source of a great deal of suffering."[19] Christ would certainly agree with Ruether about the
oppressive dimensions of male monotheism and its domination
and suppression of other forms of religious expression.

Christ's critique of what appear to be liberating images of
God is very helpful and necessary in moving us toward a fuller
biblical understanding of images and language for God. She
offers a substantial critique of what Ruether labels "God-Lan-
guage Beyond Patriarchy in the Biblical Tradition," and her
words are confrontive. Her questions should cause us to keep
pushing our analysis of God language and God imagery, as it
comes to us from our biblical tradition, to even greater critical
depths. To examine only one aspect of God language without
understanding the total biblical context in which it arose is to
have a partial image. My criticism of Christ's critique is that,
while she is dethroning the warrior, angry God, she does not
adequately provide us with images of God that reflect divine
anger or indignation with injustice. What is the appropriate
response of God to the Holocaust, to impending nuclear war,
to the rape of lands and people? This raging against injustice
must be incorporated into feminist images of God, for it is one
of many appropriate responses to the realities in the world.

Just as many Christian feminist preachers have woven equivalent female and male God images and inclusive God language

into their proclamation, many also continually work with large organizing concepts or paradigms of a liberating God. In many ways, to incorporate the strands of our tradition that point to a prophetic God, a liberating sovereign, and a God who breaks through all idolatries is a much more radical stance in Christian preaching than to articulate equivalent female God images in addition to male God images, which serves to leave patriarchal Christianity intact. "We should guard against concepts of divine androgyny that simply ratify on the divine level the patriarchal split of the masculine and the feminine."[20] To preach out of understandings that declare God's activity to be the activities of liberation—acts of prophetic confrontation of all present systems of domination and the shattering of idols of every kind and description—is much more revolutionary than the balancing of God images.

My own evolving process as woman preacher has led me to integrate both approaches to God language and imagery. I think that many women and men who preach with a feminist theological consciousness preach from a foundational place that affirms that God is a liberating, confronting presence in the world. Many of us would have left the Christian church by now if we did not believe this to be a foundational truth in our spirituality and an undergirding belief for our ministry and preaching. However, I also believe that women turn to images from their own contemporary female lives when they need to feel and know a God of compassion, comfort, and justice in their lives. Concrete images of God from female experience remind us that God acts in everyday experiences and activities of women's lives, a truth silenced and unacknowledged by most traditional God language.

Women's Experience and Naming God

This last source of God language emerges from within women's experience today, individually and collectively. Instead of women always starting our process of theologizing about God in the biblical tradition, many of us are now beginning to claim our own authority in the naming of God from our own distinctive female lives. The source of our God images and

our God language shifts from the biblical heritage as primary,
to our own lives' being another center of naming and theologizing. This is not to disregard the biblical tradition; rather it is to
suggest that it is not the first and only source of authority and
wisdom in our religious naming. This naming of God from our
own lives as women often takes artistic form. Many women
preachers are discovering that there are powerful and integrative ways to give expression to this God reality that we experience. We do our naming in dance and song, poetry and image,
and are slowly learning how to name God in new and diverse
ways. This is where I depart and go beyond what I have thus
far articulated about the present work of Christian feminist
scholars.

In *God's Fierce Whimsy,* the Mud Flower Collective speaks
to the role of the imagination in the naming of God and claims
imaging as the primary language of feminist theology:

> Feminist theology must be inductive, synthetic, and imagi-
> native. . . . Thus, images, rather than conceptual discourse
> or linear logic, are the roots of feminist theology, our pri-
> mary language. Images are not simply the first mode of our
> expression, but the most basic—and usually the most sub-
> stantive—language of feminist theology.[21]

Many women experience imaging not only as sustaining and
integrative but also as a very self-empowering process of claiming our own voices and our own experience as visionary expressions of God for our world. The power of imaging is central to
the power of women's expressed self in the world. Old ways of
naming God in concepts and abstract definitions simply are
inadequate for many religious women, including those of us who
consistently name God in our preaching. The void that many
women have felt in their search for meaningful God language
has finally pushed many of us to take our own knowing and
naming of God more seriously.

Sallie McFague, in her book *Metaphorical Theology,* distinguishes between religious language, which is the language of
images and metaphors, and theological language, which is the
language of models and concepts.[22] For too long all we have had
to draw upon is God language based on models and concepts.

Many Christian and Jewish feminists are transforming God language as we turn it more toward images and metaphors:

> What revolutionary feminists have done in their critique of the hegemony of the patriarchal model [God the Father] is to open once again the gates of the religious imagination which for too long have been locked against interpreting the divine-human relationship except in one dominant mode. . . . They are radically metaphorical, making connections most people do not make and that many find uncomfortable.[23]

The somewhat "revolutionary" nature of women's beginning with their own female lives and experiences for the naming and imaging of God is visionary indeed. My point of disagreement with McFague's assessment has to do with her belief that it is the "revolutionary feminists" who are the sole collective group of women who are departing from the tradition and turning to the authority of their own experience. I believe that countless Christian feminists and many women preachers weave together images of God from our biblical tradition and from female experience in subtle and transforming ways. Perhaps this is revolutionary in yet another way, a radical naming from within the church.

McFague, in a later book *Models of God,* is a powerful example of one woman naming God in a pastorally sensitive, prophetically confrontive way. She contends that in a nuclear age we must create and name metaphors for God that call the human community into greater responsiveness to creation. In a day when life itself is threatened, we need to name and understand God in such a way that we can no longer remain passive and detached from the incredible realities of contemporary existence. She develops images of God as mother, friend, and lover—all images that compel us to see our covenantal relationship with the Creator in an intimate way and in a socially responsible way.[24] Our traditional images for God that leave God distanced, all powerful, controlling, and all saving are not adequate images for God in a nuclear age. These images leave us passively dependent and irresponsibly disengaged from our portion of the covenant of creation and redemption. As

McFague asks us to imagine the world as God's body,[25] one cannot help but be confronted with an understanding of the divine that weaves its way into every ethical action, every activity of redemption in which one participates within our world community.

When preaching from a feminist perspective, preachers must choose how they will weave into their preaching inclusive God language and imagery. For some, the weaving will stop with the integration of equivalent female and male God images from the biblical tradition. For others, the weaving will include equivalent female/male God images from the scriptures, together with understandings of God as liberator, prophetic presence, and one who is beyond all naming. And for yet others, the weaving of inclusive God language will be a constant ever-expanding process of weaving all the liberating images we can reclaim from our biblical heritage with the powerful and new images for God and God's activity that are being born today from the depths of female experience. The images and language we use to speak of God become the initial strands of the warp threads of our weaving. Our warp threads for God are threads of *tradition,* threads of *critique,* and threads of *new imagery.*

Christology

In the context of the Christian church, issues surrounding Christology are paramount and basic to the content of preaching. If God language provides a difficult challenge to Christian feminists who preach, Christology issues pose an even deeper and penetrating challenge for those who have the responsibility of "proclaiming the gospel" in local church communities. This issue is so controversial and fragile that it is not discussed openly even among most clergywomen that I know. Perhaps issues of Christology are painful and difficult for many women because there is a strong sense in many of us that where we ultimately stand on this issue will determine whether or not we remain within the Christian church. Many of us recognize that to critique traditional christological thought is to wage a critique against the very heart of Christian doctrine and theology. Still, for many of us it is becoming increasingly painful not to give expression to the basic christological struggles we experience each time we preach. Critical feminist thought does critique traditional christological theology and doctrine, but it is oftentimes in hopes of reclaiming the deepest power of Christian faith and the most liberating dimensions of incarnational theology. As inclusive God language and imagery become a part of the warp strands of preaching from a feminist perspective, so is Christology a very basic portion of those foundational threads from which we weave our proclaimed creations.

I want to claim my own position on this issue from the onset. I am well aware that there are many women who preach regularly and who consider themselves Christian feminists, who feel no critical tension between traditional christological thought and their own theology. Those women who would consider themselves within the Christian feminist evangelical movement might be a case in point. This is not my position. As a woman preacher, I have felt a critical tension between my own Christology and the Christology of most mainline Protestant theology for several years now. I also have felt a critical tension between my own theological commitments on this issue and the christological beliefs broadly voiced in the local church communities in which I was a pastor and preacher. This is a difficult and isolating tension to live with week to week. I think that mainline Protestant churches have no idea just how many women feel this tension around Christology and have even less understanding about the impact of that tension on the content of feminist women's preaching.

In the homiletics scholarship there is once again a basic lack of awareness of any feminist theological thought and critique. In most of the literature in the field there is simply no acknowledgment that feminist critical theology even exists; there is certainly no mention of its possible impact on the preaching of women and men. Traditional assumptions about Christology persist. A statement at the beginning of Robert W. Duke's *The Sermon as God's Word* reflects this blatant disregard for feminist work: "I have omitted the more recent theological trends—process, relational, charismatic, feminist, developmental, the theology of hope, and the emerging evangelical theology—not because they are unimportant, but because they are, at this writing, still in the process of forming, maturing, or even dying.[26] This book then proceeds to explore neoorthodoxy, existentialism, liberalism, fundamentalism, Black liberation, all schools of theological thought that perpetuate traditional christological thought, with the exception of Albert Cleage's chapter on Black liberationism.

As I look critically at my own preaching theology and as I hear countless other Protestant women voice their christological concerns, these are a few of the questions I hear raised continually: How can a male Jesus of Nazareth be considered a normative model for all humanity? Can I relate any longer to the concept of savior or, more particularly, to the concept of a male savior? Is it possible to separate the historical Jesus from the Christ of faith? Is the experience of God's incarnation forever limited to one person in human history? What authority and power does Jesus' ministry have for women today?

In *Faith, Feminism, and the Christ,* Patricia Wilson-Kastner voices the overarching concern about Christology and the Christian faith in the very beginning of her book:

> But even after questions about the image of God and language about God have been adequately responded to, when the helpful dialogue is well underway, and after the past and present role of women in the church and society is explored in great depth with an eye toward a transformed figure, a vexing problem remains for Christians. No matter how one analyzes, explains, and remythologizes, at the heart of the Christian faith lies Jesus Christ, a male human being.[27]

As with my exploration of a feminist critique of traditional God language, I now want to highlight several of the sources of critique that women draw upon in search of redefinitions in relation to Christology. The sources I will suggest do not represent a minor transformation of christological thought; rather, they represent feminist critical theology that insists on new definitions and much broader understandings of incarnational theology.

Constructive/Visionary Feminist Christology
Power in Relation

One of the most profound feminist critiques concerning Christology, and one of the most insightful works in the reinterpreting and reclaiming of the historical Jesus, is found in Isabel Carter Heyward's *The Redemption of God*. Her basic contention is that until we "re-image" the work and action of the historical Jesus, we have little hope as feminists, and as a contemporary church, of understanding in a new, liberating way the meaning of the eternal Christ. If we can discern more fully what Jesus' activity and power in the world was all about, we can move closer to understanding what it means to incarnate the spirit and power of God today in our own lives. The conviction behind Heyward's work is to move Christology away from a static Christ event in history to a living reality we all are called to embody today. "To image what Jesus did instead of who he was is to lay emphasis on Jesus of Nazareth rather than on the eternal Christ. It is a way of beginning to lay the groundwork for a functional christology."[28] It is the weaving together of truths and profound insights out of the life and work of Jesus of Nazareth in such a way that the weaving illumines the limitations, power, and witness of our own lives more fully. We look at the tapestry of Jesus' life to discern, understand, and create our own tapestry more faithfully in response to God's movement in our own lives and in the world.

It is essential to understand the several foundational truths for Heyward that ground Jesus' activity in the world:

> In Jesus' relation to God, Jesus grows *with* God in love.
> . . . Jesus was responsible for his action in relation to God.
> . . . By God, with God, for God, Jesus claims his own authority of possibility in the world. By Jesus, with Jesus, through Jesus, God acts. . . . If Jesus is to be understood as "divine," "divinity" must be understood in the functional terms of choice and activity.[29]

Jesus is not God, but Jesus' activity as justice bearer, healer of pain-filled humanity, and profound relational presence embodies and incarnates God in our world. Jesus exists and lives

in the most intimate, interdependent relationship with all creation and the Creator.

For Heyward there are three fundamental features of Jesus'
relational presence and love. Those three features are intimacy,
immediacy, and passion.

Intimacy. Jesus' ministry and activity in the world were centered in a quality of mutuality. Mutuality is always rooted in an
awareness of the fundamental human similarities that connect
individual to individual, and individual to world. Jesus was
keenly in tune with his own humanness. He identified with the
needs, limitations, longings, and joys of those who shared life
with him. Jesus knows himself as a human being who, like all
human beings, is seeking to touch and be touched, move and be
moved, heal and be healed. "Intimacy is the vital condition for
Jesus' ministry."

Immediacy. Jesus' activity in the world was rooted in a ministry of presence. He was keenly aware of the past and anticipated
the future with a prophetic, visionary hopefulness; yet his being
permeated the present moment. His responsiveness to human
persons was always immediate and direct. "Jesus' life may be
best characterized by its immediacy: an urgent sense of investment in the present. Neither God nor humanity needs media-
tion. As Jesus acted immediately—without interposition—in
relation to his Abba and to his sisters and brothers, so too could
his friends act immediately in the world."

Passion. Jesus' action, his work in the world, was grounded
in the capacity for deepest solidarity. His anger, his pain, his
moments of healing, his persevering confrontations even unto
death were all in the name of solidarity with all creation. His
passion was the energy and power that always moved him into
more complex and dangerous risks on behalf of justice. "Re-
image the passion as the intense suffering of both pain and joy,
a passion which Jesus chose. . . . Jesus suffered pain not because
he was perceived to be too radical, but rather because he was
too radical to be accommodated into the present order."[30]

These features of Jesus' love and relational work in the world serve as the threads of a functional Christology, a relevant and vital incarnational theology. The *intimacy* of Jesus' work stands in stark contrast to a distanced, otherworldly Christ figure, and challenges us to claim our mutual part of the work that yet needs to be done. The *immediacy* of Jesus' presence confronts our removed mediator images of the Christ and demands that we live our own power in relation to all creation. The *passion* of Jesus' entire life reclaims for life the power of his anger, his pain, and his death, forever reminding us of the cost to all who would act on behalf of God in our world.

Radical Activity of Love

Closely related to Heyward's "power in relation" is Beverly Harrison's christological concept "radical activity of love." In Harrison's "The Power of Anger in the Work of Love," she poignantly elucidates what she feels is a major distortion in orthodox Christology.

> Orthodox Christological interpretations imply that somehow the entire meaning of Jesus' life and work is to be found in his headlong race toward Golgotha, toward crucifixion—as if he sought suffering as an end in itself. . . . I believe that this way of viewing Jesus' work robs it of its—and his—moral radicality. . . . He accepted sacrifice. But his sacrifice was for the cause of radical love. . . . Sacrifice I submit, is not a central moral goal or virtue in the Christian life. Radical acts of love expressing human solidarity and bringing mutual relationship to life—are the central virtues of the Christian moral life.[31]

Much of orthodox christological thought emerges from a distorted understanding of sacrifice. Sacrifice is often necessary in order to change unjust structures and participate in the liberation of oppressed and marginalized people, but sacrifice should never be seen as a virtue to be idolized or romanticized. Sacrifice is often the necessary repercussion of the "radical activity of love." The emphasis on sacrifice in orthodox Christology has

been particularly damaging and disempowering to women; thus
I want to encourage a further critical reflection upon it by way
of an illustration.

In the spring of 1986 I spoke to a conference of approximately
eighty United Methodist clergywomen from all over the northeastern portion of the United States. After a brief discussion
about contemporary critical feminist thought and Christology,
I showed them a poster of the *Christa.* The *Christa,* a sculptured
art piece portraying a female crucified Christ image, was created
by Edwina Sandys. From my first viewing of this sculpture in
California in 1985 until the present moment I have been deeply
troubled by this piece of art. I am not offended by the portrayal
of a female Christ figure (seen as blasphemous by many people
who have viewed it nationally). Nor am I indifferent to its
powerful depiction of women's suffering. Even though I am
deeply committed to naming women's suffering through words,
art, music, and religious symbolism, I am critical of romanticizing that suffering in ways that perpetuate it. I am increasingly
convinced that suffering has not had, and must never have, the
final say in describing and depicting the lives of women. We
must be attentive and critically evaluative of all expressions that
portray women primarily as recipients of suffering rather than
as agents of "radical acts of love."

> There are no ways around crucifixion, given the power of
> evil in the world. But as the poetic theologian of the gay
> liberation movement Sandra Browders has reminded us,
> the aim of love is not to perpetuate crucifixions, but to bring
> an end to them in a world where they go on and on and
> on! We do this through actions of mutuality and solidarity,
> not by aiming at an ethic of sacrifice.[32]

Women must be cautious and critical of any symbols, language,
or art that lingers in a romanticizing way on suffering and fails
to claim women's final passionate investment in life.

Jesus as a Parable of God

As diverse as the feminist critique of orthodox Christology
remains, perhaps the common thread that links these new

emerging christological perspectives is their overwhelming emphasis on relationality. Sallie McFague continues this emphasis as she asserts the concept and conviction that Jesus is a parable of God. Parables are built and created from metaphors, and the primary intent of metaphors is to help us make relational connections between a known reality in our lives and an unknown mystery. We look to the life and activity of Jesus, the known, to understand more fully God, the unknown. All human knowing and interpretation is metaphorical in nature; our theology, our christological insights and convictions might most creatively emerge from this manner of knowing reality. The parables of Jesus are in themselves metaphors most often connected to enabling people to understand the reign of God on earth, the love of God, or some aspect of our human-God relationship. McFague asserts that not only did Jesus speak in the language of metaphor and parable in order to help people understand the nature and activity of God, but Jesus himself was a living parable:

> A metaphor is not an ornament or illustration, but says what cannot be said in any other way; likewise, Jesus as parable of God provides us with a grid or screen for understanding God's way with us which cannot be discarded after we have translated it into concepts.

Jesus does not create our total or sole understanding of God; rather, Jesus' contribution to the fullness and breadth of our awareness of God is central. When we declare that Jesus is a parable of God, we also are affirming that Jesus is not God, for metaphors and parables point to similarities and dissimilarities, not to literal identification. And just as Jesus is a parable of God, so also others are able to be their own distinctive parables of God's activity in our world. "Metaphorical statements are never identity statements; hence, idolatry, 'Jesusolatry,' is avoided, and while we look through the story of Jesus to gain an understanding of what it means to live under God's rule, we cannot make the illegitimate move of identifying Jesus with God."

To see Jesus as a parable of God allows our Christology to be liberating and expansive. The particularities of his maleness, his moment in history, his religious heritage are now seen as expressions of his distinctive revelation of God, but they do not have universal or normative power for all people.

A parabolic Christology relativizes Jesus' particularity while universalizing the God of whom Jesus is a metaphor. Hence, openness to other manifestations and expressions of divine reality is not only encouraged but mandated.[33]

Seeing Jesus as a parable of God and recognizing our own challenge to be parables of God give us some specific clues about what faithful activity in the world might look like. Thus, it is not just that Jesus is a revelation of God; if he is a parable of God he is a particular kind of revelation of God. His activity in the world will be an assault to conventionality, a prophetic challenge to present structures, and an iconoclastic voice and presence in the face of all forms of idolatrous beliefs and living. This is what it means to be a parable; this is what it means to be the Christ.

Visions of Salvation

A final exploration in critical feminist perspectives on Christology centers around the concept of a living process of wholeness and healing. Rita Nakashima Brock, in "The Feminist Redemption of Christ," centers her discussion of Christology on salvific moments in human life that are empowering and healing. From a feminist theological perspective, she reclaims and redefines the christological construct of salvation and liberates it from orthodox patriarchal theology:

Christology takes a first-century Jewish male and makes authoritative, exclusive claims about his divinity, using writings that are already imaginative theology. . . . But the new feminist vision of existence requires radical acts of rethinking and does not rely on an absolute dogmatic certainty. . . . The foundational strength of feminism is not a self-righteous and self-sacrificing allegiance to a central image or a totalitarian ideology, but a clear statement of experienced oppression.

Women have experienced oppression at the hands of a patriarchal church and as a result of the dualistic worldview perpetuated by the Christian church. Our experiences of pain and suffering and our empowered responses to that oppression become the context for salvific action. Salvation is not that which happens to us when we are "saved" from ourselves by a mediating savior; rather salvation is something we do with each other in community. Salvation does not happen once and for all time; it happens over and over again in life:

> The feminist Christian commitment is not to a savior who redeems us by bringing God to us. Our commitment is to love ourselves and others into wholeness. Our commitment is to a divine presence with us here and now, a presence that works through the mystery of our deepest selves and our relationships, constantly healing us and nudging us toward a wholeness of existence, we only fitfully know.

Brock affirms what other feminist theologians have so persistently claimed—that relationality is the key to this healing and transformation. It is the sheer power of our presence with each other, through suffering and through joy, that gives birth to healing and ultimate human wholeness. Jesus knew this truth, and his activity in the world reflected it completely. He is known to us as healer, friend, companion, and loving presence—all ways of knowing and being known that lead to moments of human transformation and empowerment. He is only one example, however, for we too must embody that healing presence as faithfully in our context as Jesus lived it in his. Brock's emphasis on salvation as a christological concept is a powerful way for women to appropriate the Christ event as an event of human healing and the embodiment of the human vision of wholeness. Her christological concept is not exclusive and seeks to empower women to claim the moments in their own lives and in their own activity in the world where they participate clearly in salvation. "We redeem Christ when we recognize the images of Jesus Christ that reflect our hunger for healing wholeness and claim those images as resources for hope."[34]

As I review the diversity and richness of feminist theological

thought in relation to Christology, and clarify the repercussions
of this work for contemporary preachers, I am aware of several
critical recurring themes and implications: Whether one looks
to the healing presence of Jesus, his radical acts of love, his
power of relation, or his revolutionary parabolic acts, reclaiming Jesus from a feminist perspective is always rooted in relationality. It is the power of his relational presence in the world
that was transforming. It is the intimacy of his communion with
God and the passion and intimacy of his solidarity with the
human family that made him a living parable of divine power
and a transformer of existent reality. This relational power, this
presence, is at the heart of preaching from a feminist perspective
and becomes the soul of our preaching. It is not Jesus' special
set-apartness, nor his privileged relationship with the Creator,
nor his normative humanity that will be the source of christological content in preaching from a feminist perspective. When we
preach about Jesus, it must be about his humanness, his revolutionary and prophetic actions in response to oppressive structures, his healing interactions with the broken and wounded,
and his eternal unwillingness to be named or understood as the
only revelation of God. When women and men speak of the
Christ in their preaching, they need to be clear that they speak
of a power among us today. When we ask ourselves, Who is the
Christ? our preaching should point us to each other in community. Wherever people live in the power of relation, or perform
radical acts of love, or give witness to a transforming love, there
is the Christ! Feminist Christology is a radical shift from a sole
focus on the historical Jesus to the living presence of God in our
midst and within us. Jesus' ministry has revelatory power for us
today, but it cannot have exclusive and ultimate authority.
Women particularly must look to their own healing and relational power, their prophetic voices and naming, and their thor-
oughgoing critique of the tradition as sources of their own
authority. Authority and power are aspects of being in the world
that each person must claim for her/himself; it is not a quality
we receive from another, not even Jesus, who has been called the
Christ.

Before leaving this section on Christology, I raise two major
concerns for future reflection and work within the Christian

church in general and within feminist religious circles in particular. The first concern has to do with Christology questions and the Black church experience. It has become clear to me that the critique of orthodox Christology from a feminist perspective remains a predominantly white middle-class women's critique. There are exceptions to be sure, but the majority of work done in this area of feminist Christology has come from a very particular group of women within the Christian tradition. I am also aware that the feminist critique that I have articulated in these pages appears to be in direct conflict with strong, traditional christological messages alive and well in the Black church. Mervyn A. Warren says in *Black Preaching,* "At the core of contemporary Black preaching throbs a dominant Christocentrism."[35]

In the same conference I referred to earlier (United Methodist clergywomen from the northeastern portion of this country), I was confronted and challenged by a Black woman after my presentation on Christology. I had alluded to the fact that there is a different theological agenda existent in the Black church and that Black women preachers appear to have a christological viewpoint very different from that of many white women who are preaching. This woman concurred with my reference and wished that I had spent more time exploring this point of contrast. Katie Geneva Cannon, in "The Emergence of Black Feminist Consciousness," speaks about this issue when she says:

> Knowing the Jesus stories of the New Testament helps Black women be aware of the bad housing, overworked mothers, underworked fathers, functional illiteracy, and malnutrition that continue to prevail in the Black community. . . . Jesus provides the necessary soul for liberation.[36]

Jesus has been a strong source of liberation and freedom for many Black women; thus the struggles around Christology appear to be of a very different nature for women with such heritage in the Black church. Several of the Black women in the conference affirmed that they make no distinction between God and Jesus, a distinction that is at the heart of much feminist critique Christology.

After reading *Those Preachin' Women,* edited by Ella Pearson Mitchell, I was confronted again with the reality of differ-

ences. In the majority of sermons in that volume, very different
christological assumptions abound than one would presently
find in many white Protestant women's sermons, particularly
those women influenced by feminist theology. For many Black
women preachers Jesus is clearly Lord; there is no clear distinction between Jesus the Christ and God. Christ is still the one
who calls for obedience and is the ultimate suffering servant.
Jesus is a constant and ever-present companion and friend.[37]
These understandings of both the historical Jesus and the Christ
of faith appear to be substantially different from many of the
christological struggles that appear in my own life and preaching and in the lives and preaching of many of my feminist, white
Protestant sisters. Perhaps the place of unity exists wherever
Jesus is seen as liberator and champion of the oppressed and as
prophetic agent in the world, confronting all structures and
systems that divide and oppress the human community. White
women also have used the Jesus stories as sources for their fight
for liberation and equality.

I raise this issue because I believe it is essential for all women
to keep claiming the particularities of their own theological
agenda and because I believe this point of contrast has not been
fully tapped as a rich resource for the refinement of women's
entire christological thought. This is a powerful theological
agenda between and among all feminist and Black womanist
preachers.

And finally, I note a concern about the relationship of our
christological positions and beliefs to anti-Semitism and narrow
religious parochialism. The Christian community is only beginning to take seriously the implications of our Christology for
communication and connections with global religious perspectives. Feminist theologians are strongly confronting the church
with the fact that its total emphasis on Jesus as messiah and
savior has been profoundly destructive to Jewish/Christian dialogue. Sallie McFague says:

> If Jesus is understood as *a* parable of God, one which
> Christians claim is a true one, then other religions can
> make the claim that they also contain metaphorical expres-
> sions of divine reality. In spite of the difficulties in ad-

judicating alternative and conflicting claims, to deny such possibilities is to limit God to a "tribal" status and ultimately to make an idol of Christianity.[38]

Dorothee Sölle is even more confrontive about the kind of Christology that pervades American culture and society, describing U.S. society as "christo-fascist," "a society bent in the name of a false Christ upon a monolithic-nonpluralistic, intolerant, arrogant, and genocidal-image of what is moral, valuable, beautiful, and worthy of life."[39] This is a stinging critique of an issue long ignored. We must look critically at our Christologies as women who preach and teach in terms of their oppressive nature not only in relation to sexism but also in relation to every other structure of oppression that traditional christological thought has perpetuated.

As a feminist Christian woman I continually struggle with Christology, and the struggle is magnified when I preach. There is a constant struggle to redeem the Christ of faith as a living reality and possibility for contemporary community. The strands of the warp threads with which we weave our proclamation must integrate this new vision into the preaching craft. I with this challenge:

> I suggest that female Christians, black Christians, poor Christians, and gay/lesbian Christians participate in the perpetuation of our own oppression insofar as we allow our visions and energies to be drawn toward a heavenly man and away from our human situation as sisters and brothers, by fixing our attention on the spiritual accomplishments of a divine Savior rather than on the spiritual possibilities of a concerted human commitment that can be inspired by the Jesus story . . . a story of human faith, human love, and human possibility as the agency of divine movement in history.[40]

Biblical Hermeneutics

The interwoven quality of biblical hermeneutics and preaching is self-evident. The issue that is not as clear to most of the scholars and theologians in the field of homiletics is the need for a feminist interpretation of the Bible. As long as biblical texts are primary sources for preaching the word of God, issues surrounding the nature or method of biblical interpretation are critical and central. As women and men choose the texture and nature of the warp threads for their weaving proclamations, they must ask themselves several key questions in relation to biblical hermeneutics: What authority do I give the Bible in my own life of faith and spirituality? What is the nature of this authority? How do the scriptures intersect with my own life as a contemporary woman, a contemporary man? How do the scriptures serve to perpetuate my own oppression and the oppression of others? How do they serve as sources of liberation? Are there texts that simply should not be proclaimed or preached, texts that are not able to be redeemed in terms of feminist biblical critique?

These are only a few of the questions that women and men preaching from a feminist perspective struggle with daily in their search to proclaim a liberating word of God. The critique of feminist biblical scholars and theologians in terms of biblical interpretation and scriptural authority is severe and thorough. There is an ever-increasing amount of feminist scholarship in this area of theological reflection, demonstrating the magnitude and the need of such critical thought. The critique allows no assumptions about the "objectivity" of the biblical text to go unquestioned and unchallenged. "Not only is scripture interpreted by a long line of men and proclaimed in patriarchal churches, it is also authored by men, written in androcentric language, reflective of religious male experience, selected and transmitted by male religious leadership."[41] Given this reality, the emergence of a feminist biblical hermeneutics is not only a necessary corrective, but is absolutely essential if inclusive preachers are to continue to give the scriptures any relevant authority in their own lives and in the life of their preaching.

As homiletics scholarship fails to address issues of God language and Christology from a feminist perspective, it is equally inattentive to the entire body of scholarship now known as feminist biblical interpretation or feminist biblical hermeneutics. Traditional homiletics theology persists in making the same unexamined assumptions about the absolute authority of the Bible that it has made for centuries.

As a case in point, I offer a feminist challenge to the four basic underlying assumptions about biblical interpretation found in William D. Thompson's *Preaching Biblically.* [42]

1. *God is predictably omnipotent, eternal, omniscient, and true. God always acts among us creatively and redemptively.* My critique comes at two levels in response to this first presupposition. The first has to do with language. Most feminist scholars and preachers have strong commitments to move away from language like omnipotence, omniscience, and exclusively transcendent images and qualities for the nature and activity of God. This is not a God of relationality and intimacy, but a distanced God, "holy other" in relation to the human community. The second level of criticism has to do with the activity of God. Are women and others who are oppressed to believe and assume that God's action in our world is always redemptive and creative? If God shares in our life together, then perhaps God also suffers in moments of human suffering, experiences powerlessness in moments of human bondage, and does not move in moments of human apathy and indifference. For most feminists, God is not a far-removed, eternally benevolent being, but a sacred presence among and within us, more than we are but intricately interwoven with all human activity.

2. *There is continuity in human nature and experience.* Contemporary people can totally identify with the humanity of the Israelites and the humanity of persons in the New Testament. There is no real discontinuity in who human persons have been throughout history. My basic criticism of this presupposition is that it fails to acknowledge that the scriptures primarily document and describe male experience. Even when the narrative accounts center around women, the account almost exclusively reflects male authorship and male interpretation. The authority of the scriptures becomes problematic when the actual biblical narratives do not reflect half the human race's experience.

3. *There is unity and ultimate authority in biblical revelation.* The interpretive enterprise proceeds on the general presupposition that the Bible contains God's authoritative word for us.

This is precisely the point in question for feminists. Feminists are questioning both the content of biblical revelation (who has declared scripture God's revelation in the first place?) and the ultimate authority this "interpreted revelation" has for our lives as contemporary women and men. It has become clear to a number of feminists that many biblical texts contribute to the oppression of marginalized people. These texts frequently perpetuate a kind of theology that serves the powerful and reinforces the present power structures. Are women to proclaim texts and messages that we fundamentally perceive to be oppressive? "Faithfulness to the struggle of women for liberation requires a theological judgment and an insistence that oppressive patriarchal texts and sexist traditions cannot claim the authority of divine revelation."[43] Christian feminists no longer assume that the Bible has ultimate authority, nor do they agree that all texts should be understood as God's revelation.

4. *Christian experience is necessary.* The interpreter of biblical texts and the preacher of biblical faith must participate in the community of faith which has produced, preserved, and now lives by the power of the scriptures, and must have a personal experience of redemption of Jesus Christ. Both presuppositions from a feminist perspective are problematic. First, many feminist Christian scholars and preachers are quite aware that women did not produce the Bible. Even though the entire community of faith, the early church, was the context out of which the scriptures emerged, the canon was produced, authored, and sealed by men. Thus, when we require that all preachers participate in the community of faith, to what community do we refer and whose experience does it represent? Second, this presupposition does not take into account new feminist understandings of the historical Jesus or the Christ of faith. Many women no longer assume that Jesus Christ is savior for them, or at least not in the traditional understandings of what savior means in Christian theology, and therefore they question the entire validity of the concept.

In contrast to the traditional presuppositions for interpretation just discussed for biblical preaching, Elisabeth Schüssler Fiorenza proposes a feminist method of biblical hermeneutics that affirms a very different set of presuppositions. She begins development of this method in her book *In Memory of Her: A Feminist Theological Reconstruction of Christian Origins,* but it is illuminated systematically in her more recent book *Bread Not Stone.* Her method of biblical interpretation rests on four foundational assumptions: (1) The Bible has within it both an androcentric worldview and a message of human liberation. (2) The Bible contains both texts that portray women's suffering and oppression and texts that affirm women's power. (3) Feminist biblical hermeneutics begins with women's experience and makes no pretense of being objective or value free. (4) Feminist biblical hermeneutics involves "uncovering lost traditions, and correcting mistranslations, and peeling away androcentric scholarship."[44] It is a method of interpretation that seeks to critique both the biblical texts themselves and the traditional scholarship that has interpreted them.

The following model of feminist biblical interpretation is most fully developed by Fiorenza, yet is also the result of the collective search and work of many women who no longer find traditional biblical interpretation adequate or faithful:

> A feminist critical interpretation of the Bible cannot take as its point of departure the normative authority of the biblical archetype, but must begin with women's experience in their struggle for liberation. . . . The hermeneutical center of such a feminist biblical interpretation . . . is the *ekklesia gynaikon,* or women-church, the movement of self-identified women and women-identified men in biblical religion.[45]

1. *A feminist critical interpretation begins with a hermeneutics of suspicion rather than with a hermeneutics of consent and affirmation.*[46] To begin biblical interpretation with suspicion rather than consent means that women and men must never unconditionally accept its authority or its initial message without deeper, more thorough critique and investigation. This includes being suspicious about previous interpretations, most often exclusively proposed by male scholars. It means we approach the biblical text with a critical lens through which we evaluate both the meaning it conveys and the purpose it serves. As women and men, we must acknowledge how historical and

contemporary communities have used biblical texts to justify
and sanctify every description and kind of human oppression.
Robert W. Duke, in *The Sermon as God's Word,* says, "One
comes to the text and listens, setting aside, as far as humanly
possible, all one's own questions and bracketing one's own assumptions."[47] This statement epitomizes an opposite approach
from a hermeneutics of suspicion, for it is absolutely necessary
that feminist women who preach and men committed to feminist biblical interpretation bring *all* their deepest and best questions to the task of hermeneutics. It means that we realize, even
after we have read the best of biblical commentaries, that we still
do not have access to women's insights, interpretations, and
wisdom concerning any given text. It means that we do not
assume the texts we approach for exegesis and then for proclamation necessarily have an underlying message of liberation and
human wholeness. Rather, a hermeneutics of suspicion assumes
that we often must look beneath the text, through the text, and
behind the text to recover a faithful message of God's revelatory
action in the world.

Feminist hermeneutics of suspicion has enabled many women
scholars to reclaim, reinterpret, and reconstruct many of the
biblical texts in order to unearth a truthful and ultimately liberating message about women's lives, for the lives and work of
women and men today. The important work of Phyllis Trible,
in her *God and the Rhetoric of Sexuality* and *Texts of Terror,*
is a clear example of feminist biblical scholarship that proceeds
from a hermeneutics of suspicion. In these books, Trible uses
rhetorical criticism, a form of literary criticism where the text
itself is the clue to interpretation.[48] Trible's careful attention to
the details of biblical texts has led her to new discoveries about
the power of women and life-giving images of female experience
within the scriptures. In addition, she has documented discoveries of overwhelming violence, brutalization, and invisibility of
other women within biblical narratives. Her work embodies and
fundamentally affirms one of the basic assumptions behind feminist biblical hermeneutics. The Bible has within it both an androcentric worldview reflected in "texts of terror" and a
liberating message in "God and the rhetoric of sexuality."

2. *While a historically adequate translation of the Bible brings*

to the fore the sexist-patriarchal as well as the feminist-inclusive character of biblical texts, a hermeneutics of proclamation assesses the Bible's theological significance and power for the contemporary community of faith.[49] A feminist hermeneutics of proclamation analyzes the impact and power certain texts will have when preached in a contemporary community of faith. A hermeneutics of suspicion determines how women and men will approach and understand the text. A hermeneutics of proclamation determines how women and men will articulate and share the text or whether a given text should be given an authoritative voice. "The whole canon is to be taken seriously, especially because of the possibility of the Bible's use as a tool for the oppression of women. But it is not considered to function as the Word of God, evoking consent or faith, if it contributes to the continuation of racism, sexism, and classism."[50]

A feminist hermeneutics of proclamation takes the responsibility and task of the preacher very seriously. The preacher must not only be attentive to the blatant and obvious exclusive language issues, sexist illustrations and stories, and androcentric attitudes in the biblical texts themselves, but she or he must also evaluate the impact of the content of biblical texts for particular social, political, ethnic-racial, and economic contexts. A feminist hermeneutics of proclamation must evaluate everything that is proclaimed from the biblical text in a commitment to eradicate messages that perpetuate oppression.

A hermeneutics of proclamation, attuned to feminist values and commitments and additional liberation struggles, must also question such basic aspects of Christian preaching as following the lectionary. Who selected the texts that are present in the lectionary? Who determines which texts will be included and which will be absent? "Preachers of liberation must not forget that lectionaries are a selection which reflects the prevailing tradition of the church, and that therefore they must be seen with the necessary 'ideological suspicion,' and corrected accordingly."[51] This critical method of reflecting on what is appropriate in terms of proclamation is in direct conflict with the conviction held by many preachers and scholars in homiletics that all texts must be preached and the preacher has the responsibility to put aside any personal biases that would prevent her

or his dealing with any of the biblical texts. A feminist hermeneutics of proclamation, as the hermeneutics of suspicion also
suggests, does not give final and ultimate authority to the biblical text alone. Rather, the ultimate authority becomes whether
the biblical text is liberating and redemptive.

3. *A feminist hermeneutics of proclamation must be balanced
by a critical hermeneutics of remembrance that recovers* all *biblical traditions through a historical-critical reconstruction of biblical history from a feminist perspective.* [52] A feminist hermeneutics
of remembrance seeks to reconstruct and remember our biblical
traditions in such a way that the voices, stories, and power of
our foresisters become available to the contemporary faith community. It is a hermeneutics that refuses to allow androcentric
texts to have the final word about the contributions and the roles
of women in the Judeo-Christian past. It is in remembering
these women's stories, their struggles, and their moments of
power and influence that we find inspiration and strength for
our work today. A feminist hermeneutics of remembrance, however, does not reclaim and reconstruct just those texts and stories about women when they were influential or central, but also
the texts and stories of women in the Bible that reflect the total
victimization of women at the hands of a patriarchal society.

In addition to Trible's contribution to the hermeneutics of
suspicion, her work also enriches a hermeneutics of remembrance. In her *God and the Rhetoric of Sexuality* she reclaims
and reconstructs several biblical texts. She reclaims the Genesis
story from its totally patriarchal interpretation as she uses the
text itself to reinterpret the position and role of Eve in the
narrative creation story. She reclaims the Song of Songs as a
book focused on female experience. She examines and celebrates
the independence and power of both Ruth and Naomi in the
book of Ruth:

> Clearly, the patriarchal stamp of scripture is permanent.
> But just as clearly, interpretation of its content is forever
> changing, since new occasions teach new duties and con-
> texts alter texts, liberating them from frozen construc-
> tions.[53]

Equally powerful is Trible's work in *Texts of Terror.* Here also she makes a monumental contribution to a feminist hermeneutics of remembrance, although this time her intent is to recover the hidden stories of women who have clearly been brutalized, raped, and violated. These stories are devastating to read and to re-member into our biblical heritage. But it is only in remembering, and never forgetting, that the experiences of these women have the chance to empower women and men today to struggle against the same androcentric worldview and dominant structures that continue to oppress and victimize women today. Perhaps preaching from these texts and declaring their devastating truth about patriarchal culture would be prophetic indeed. "If art imitates life, scripture likewise reflects it in both holiness and horror. [Sad stories] . . . by enabling insight . . . may inspire repentance."[54] Trible then proceeds to call to remembrance such stories as the rejection of Hagar in the book of Genesis, the rape of Tamar in 2 Samuel, the mutilation of the unnamed concubine from Bethlehem in Judges, and the slaying of the unnamed daughter of Jephthah in Judges.

As a feminist, I have come to understand the incredible importance of the act of remembering. Not only is it an essential in the task of biblical hermeneutics and preaching, but it is a central act of faith in gatherings of women. In recent years I have attended very few gatherings of religious women where acts of remembering our foresisters have not been central to the liturgical and celebrational life of the community. Women know all too well the silenced nature of women's experience and women's stories, and are becoming increasingly committed to giving a voice and an honored place to those who have gone before us. This act of remembering, whether it happens in our preaching, our songs, our litanies, our dances, or our symbolic acts together is a faithful act of proclamation and a foundational act in feminist spirituality.

The clergywomen's conference about which I have spoken throughout this chapter also illustrates this affirmation about the act of remembrance. The conference opened with a liturgical celebration in which three women "remembered women from the past." Each time the group gathered, candles were lighted, and we paused to remember women who had gone before us. A song that became the primary gathering song of the conference was a song of remembering. This song highlights in a poignant way the strengthening power that is available to women when we re-member our contemporary lives with the lives of other women.

> Oh, I'm steppin' out, steppin' out on the promises.
> Oh, I'm steppin' out, steppin' out all the way.
> Oh, I'm steppin' out, stepping' out on the promises,
> I'm living tomorrow today!
>
> There are women who share their stories.
> There are women who shed their tears.
> There are women who shelter our feelings, and
> There are women who soften our fears.
>
> Oh, our sisters have come before us,
> The hags and spinsters and crones.
> Great processions of ancients have called us,
> Singing "Stand tall, you're not alone."
>
> There are voices from the past and present,
> Miriam, Deborah, Harriet Tubman too.
> Sister Teresa, Alice Walker, and others,
> Singing, "Join us; the journey's for you."
>
> Yes, we're going on, moving on with God's vision,
> Making clear for the whole world to see
> Peace and justice and love and equality,
> So our daughters will be whole and free.[55]

In our feminist hermeneutics and our proclamations we do, in fact, re-member our communities when women and men make these women living realities and reclaim these women as companions for our journey now.

> A feminist hermeneutics of remembrance proposes theoretical models for historical reconstructions that place women in the center of biblical community and theology. . . . The history and theology must not be allowed to cancel out the memory of the struggle, life, and leadership of biblical women who spoke and acted in the power of the Spirit.[56]

4. *Historical reconstructions of women's biblical history need to be supplemented by a hermeneutics of creative actualization . . . seeks to retell biblical stories from a feminist perspective, to reformulate biblical visions and injunctions in the perspective of the discipleship of equals, to create narrative amplifications of the feminist remnants that have survived in patriarchal texts.* [57] For centuries the Christian church has found artistic and creative ways of appropriating and expressing the biblical message. This has been done through dance, poetry, drama, and visual art. Christian communities have often taken great liberty to express biblical texts in ways that have enlivened them and made them relevant for particular contexts. A feminist hermeneutics of creative actualization claims this liberty for women and for the distinctive ways women have chosen and will choose in the future to express the biblical stories, wisdom, and faithful revelations of the spirit of God.

A feminist hermeneutics of creative actualization, not unlike a hermeneutics of proclamation, is the embodying and expressing of the results of our biblical work and interpretations. It is the intuitive, imaginative expressions of women as they seek not only to hear the stories of their foresisters, but also to enflesh those stories with movement, ritual, and art. It is here in feminist hermeneutics where women also realize that interpretation involves creative naming. Renita J. Weems, in *Just a Sister Away,* addresses this issue of naming and creative actualization:

> *Just a Sister Away* attempts to combine the best of the fruits of feminist biblical criticism with its passion for reclaiming and reconstructing the stories of biblical women, along with the best of the Afro-American oral tradition, with its gifts for story-telling and its love for drama. [58]

The power and creativity of the imagination must be claimed in behalf of women's stories and herstory. It is a power not unknown to preaching, yet women must claim it as a resource for the expression of their own female experience, their own female truths about life and faith.

Robert Young, in *Religious Imagination,* makes a strong case for the primary role of imagination in the task and act of preaching. Imagination probes connections within creation, and is the lively heart of preaching. It is beyond the intellect and is almost mystical. Religious imagination infuses us with life and keeps us alive.[59] A feminist hermeneutics of creative actualization depends on the power of imagination and inspiration, recognizing that our contemporary interpretations and embodiments of God's presence among us are truly revelatory for our time. Our acts of creative actualization become an essential way women claim their own visions and their own naming for the proclamation of the new horizons of God's activity.

Critique Transforms Craft

I believe the preaching act and craft is being transformed by the vision and critique of feminist Christian women. The limitations and idolatry of traditional God language are being challenged, the patriarchal biases behind traditional christological thought and doctrine are being named and confronted, and scripture no longer has unquestioned authority in the lives of many who preach. The warp threads, those that provide the foundational strands for the task of weaving a new kind of proclamation, are emerging as threads of distinctive vision and prophetic insight.

Only a few years ago, critical feminist theology was still a rare phenomenon. It has now become a substantial body of scholastic theological thought. Its critique confronts every facet of religious life. No longer does critical feminist theology simply react or respond to the scholarship that it critically evaluates, but it has moved on to construct and create a new theology of its own. Christian feminists who preach draw upon this vast body of scholarship in order to reweave and change the field of homiletics and the art of preaching. Each woman and man who preaches from a feminist consciousness and commitment must weave the strands of feminist theological critique with the strands of the sociopolitical context in which she or he proclaims a message of faith. These distinctive warp strands, integrated and blended together, create new theologies, new liberating messages, and new possibilities for preaching in the Christian church today.

The social gospel movement emerged as a distinctive phe-

nomenon in Christian preaching around 1875. There are important and relevant points of contrast between the social gospel
movement and the critique of feminist Christian theology today
that provide a distinctive vision for Christian ministry and
preaching. Preachers in that era began to address their preaching explicitly to the issues of social and political concern in their
day. This was a radical change in the content and purpose of
Christian preaching. This period in American history and in the
evolution of preaching influenced the craft and meaning of
preaching for all the years that have followed. The question of
how much a sermon should address "political and social issues"
is still a very poignant one in homiletics classes and in the
week-to-week decisions that preachers make about proclamation.

I have come to appreciate greatly the impact of that "social
gospel" movement, for it still exists as a kind of "silent con-
science" of much of mainline Protestant preaching. I have,
however, also come to understand some of its limitations. In
retrospect, there are theologians and scholars who have critiqued the social gospel movement as having been narrow-
focused and somewhat ineffective in its ability to bring about
any kind of social and political transformation. The main focus
of the social gospel movement remained on issues of industrial-
ization, the rights of the working class, and growing economic
problems nationally. Henry F. May, in *Protestant Churches and
Industrial America,* offers a critique of the movement when he
says: Conservatives were not really changed in their economic
values for labor itself was often more radical and did not accept
the message of the social gospel. It was a time when churches
preached charity, not justice. Progressive social Christianity
had its greatest influence on the progressive middle class, but it
did fail to attract labor support or convert conservatives.[60] Even
though social gospel preaching was a tremendous break with
traditional understandings of preaching in that era, even though
it challenged much of the existent Christian theology, its impact
was significant, but also limited. Others have also criticized the
movement for never fully integrating issues of racial exploitation and oppression into the content and focus of social gospel
preaching.

The social gospel movement set a precedent for prophetic preaching and the commitment to weave together issues of political and social significance and issues of religious commitment. Preachers whose preaching is informed by the revolutionary ideas and convictions of feminist vision stand in a long tradition of Christian preachers striving to be prophetic. Yet it is at the point of the narrow focus of the social gospel movement that I want to assert a very strong belief: Feminist vision and its impact on preaching is a new movement for our time. Contrasted to the narrow focus of the social gospel movement, feminist vision at its finest leaves few issues unaddressed. Radical feminism sees as its agenda for transformation and justice a vision intended to be inclusive of every issue that affects the lives of the human family. Feminist vision is not progressive or liberal; it is radical and revolutionary. The Christian church has yet to know what kind of impact the preaching of feminist vision will have on its own life and the life and structures of our larger society and world.

Judith L. Hoehler, in "The Preacher as Prophet," talks about the prophetic role and vision of preaching:

> It is the prophet who compels the church to be true to its mission as an agent of healing for *all* the world, not just for those within its doors. . . . We are not the creators of truth; rather we are bearers, revealers, witnesses to the truth, which stands over against us and judges and redeems us just as it does our hearers. . . . The function of prophetic preaching is to bring about change.[61]

I have attempted to outline the nature and essence of feminist theological critique as best I experience and understand it. It is a vision that both judges and redeems us. At the heart and center of Christian feminist preaching are the warp strands of transformation.

5

The Weft of Vision:
Threads of Global Feminism

The third kind of Plain Weave is known as "weft-surface," or "weft face," fabric because in this only the weft shows and the warp is set so far apart that the weft packs down between the warp threads. The warp can be plain and uninteresting, since it does not show, but it should be strong. A design should be planned in a series of interesting horizontal weft stripes. . . . Vertical stripes may be formed by using first a weft of one color and then a weft of a second color, these being alternated regularly. Weft-surface cloth is used for decorative mats, panels, striped wall hangings, and rugs. It is the kind of texture made by the Navajo Indians in their tapestry rugs.[1]

I remember you weaving your beautiful rug by the kerosene lamp. Your hands deftly moved along the strands mystically creating a design that slowly evolved with each new row. Sometimes I would come to visit while you were gathering those special herbs that transformed each skein of carefully carded wool into hues that only nature provides. Patiently you would answer my questions "What plants are they?" "Where do they come from?" "What are their names in English? . . . in Navaho?" I envied your knowledge of all that was mysterious to me. You were the magician that created rugs so beautiful from seemingly very little. Your weaving spoke a language of its own that needed no interpretation. All the magic, all the beauty had already been transformed through you. There are many legends that you have told me (as you sat

at the loom) of how things came to be. As I listened the rug
seemed to take in all that you spoke. You became a part of
what you made, for in it was your beauty, your wisdom, your
pride.[2]

This Navajo poem speaks about the beauty, wisdom, and vision
of weaving. It is an art form and expression that cannot be fully
analyzed or explained. The weaving itself speaks a message all
its own. The weaving embodies the hopes, skills, and deepest
longings of the weaver.

Weft-faced Preaching

In the actual act of weaving, after one has placed the vertical
warp strands on the loom, one is ready to begin the creation of
weaving. One must select the color and texture of the weft
strands that will run horizontally across the warp. An important
decision must be made at this point in the weaving process.
Depending on the specific pattern of weave one chooses, either
the warp threads will ultimately show through more predominantly in the weaving or the weft threads will be more pro-
nounced. The weaving described in this chapter might be
described as "weft-faced." This simply means that the weft
strands, interwoven with the warp strands, are the threads that
are most prominent in the finished weaving. "Weft-faced weaving: A fabric with the weft so closely packed or beaten in that
the warp does not show, as in tapestry."[3] I want to suggest that
"weft-faced," or visionary, preaching is the kind of preaching
most needed in our day and most consistent with the justice
mandates of the Christian gospel.

In relation to the preaching craft in particular, I believe that
preaching from a feminist perspective might best be described
as "weft-faced" weaving. Instead of the strands of the tradition
being those that dominate, I want to explore what the content
and vision of preaching might be if threads of transformation
dominated the entire preaching creation. In this chapter, I will
give expression to many of those strands of feminist transformation and visioning that permeate our larger American culture
and, to a growing degree, our religious institutions. A commit-

ment that I clarified in Chapter 4 on the warp of tradition, I want to reiterate in this chapter on the weft of feminist vision. I do not see feminist vision as reforming but rather as a thorough and transformative vision that would leave the world a much different place were it to come into being.

Another point of clarification is needed. In the last chapter I attempted to describe various strands of feminist theological thought that pose a major critique of traditional God language, Christology, and biblical hermeneutics. I chose these three areas of theology because they are so basic to the preaching message and craft. I do not want to create a false dichotomy by suggesting that *critique* is also not *vision.* It is very clear to me that in feminist theological thought, critique is certainly also visionary thought. Feminist theologians have clearly moved beyond reactive work and are suggesting new ways of understanding and naming God, Christ, and the authority and revelatory power of the Bible. Even though much of that chapter was visionary, my intent was to point to some of the painful tension points for feminist women and men who are preaching within the Christian tradition. My hope was to give voice and expression to hidden conflicts often not discussed or acknowledged in the field of homiletics.

In this chapter, I want to move beyond the boundaries of Christianity and the sole realm of feminist theology into wider circles of feminist vision. These myriad voices of feminist transforming vision are reaching into the heart and content of preaching. These strands of vision will influence how we understand preaching done from a feminist perspective.

Inadequacy of Present Homiletical Vision

In relation to vision, I have been struggling to understand why there is so little visionary thought in homiletics literature today. Many of the scholars in the field offer various critiques of the preaching task in its present form. These critiques, however, offer little new visionary thought about the content and life-changing dimension of preaching for today. In fact, most of these voices of critique seem to be repetitive of the critique of preaching that has been lifted up periodically for centuries. The critiques express an indictment of the preacher as archaic and irrelevant, criticism of the preacher as primary symbol of the establishment, and despair at the lack of visionary preaching.[4]

Even though I would probably agree with many of the critiques that are offered today by white male scholars, I am not in agreement with most of their suggested solutions. The suggested solutions range from increased "biblical preaching," to a reclaiming of the traditional authority of the preacher, to suggestions of creative methods of sermon delivery. Very few preachers or homileticians suggest a serious critique of the content and transforming vision of preaching. Most scholars would agree that preaching needs to have a prophetic edge to it, but they spend little time articulating a vision. We need more preachers or scholars in the field of homiletics to give honest and full expression to that which motivates their voice and their message. It is my intent to do just that, to express strands of a vision that are motivating and inspiring Christian feminist preachers.

In many mainline Protestant churches, it is obvious to most preachers that the traditional authority of the preacher and the sermon is in question by both laity and clergy. It is also painfully clear to many preachers that those who preach from a fundamentalist, or evangelical, persuasion are filling the churches to overflowing. In the midst of this kind of ambiguous reality about preaching, women are choosing to preach in increasing numbers throughout the United States. I believe this has to do with a sense of vision and possibility that women feel about the preaching craft and its power to make an impact on the world as we now experience and know it. This may be a very bold assertion, but I believe it to be true. I also believe that many women are expectant and hopeful about the craft and act of preaching because it gives them an opportunity to name reality and faith experience in ways that have not always been available to them. This is precisely the point where I believe feminist women have a great deal to say about the present and future understanding of preaching. There are strands of transforming vision for our world that emerge from feminist thought, music, art, and spirituality that could shape the heart and soul of Christian preaching. Elisabeth Schüssler Fiorenza affirms:

> The danger exists that the homily will not articulate the experience of God as the rich and pluriform experience of God's people, but that the male preacher will articulate his own experience . . . as the experience of God *par excellence.* What is limited and particular to his experience will be proclaimed as universal and paradigmatic for everyone.[5]

It is time that preaching reflect much more than just the experience of male preachers; it is time that the field and art of homiletics take seriously the new strands of transforming feminist vision.

Vision as Naming and Action

There are many ways to speak about feminist vision, the process of articulating it aloud and giving it expression in our world. Carol Christ, in *Diving Deep and Surfacing,* uses the concept of "spiritual quest" to organize her thoughts and insights about women's religious and spiritual experiences and their perceptions and insights about transforming vision. More particularly, she speaks about women's need to name their own reality and tell their own stories.

> As women begin to name the world for themselves not only will they create new life possibilities for women, they will also upset the world order that has been taken for granted for centuries. . . . The subordination of women not only has been taken for granted by philosophers and poets whose writings have shaped Western consciousness, but the assumption of women's secondary status also has influenced philosophers' and poets' perceptions of the nature of authority and hierarchy. and of the relation of spirit and flesh, humanity and nature, body and soul.[6]

This is not to suggest that everything about a woman's perspective and experience is ideal or visionary. It is simply to say that women must learn to value their own reality deeply, articulate it clearly, and believe that the visions of life and faith that many women share have transforming power.

Weft-faced weaving, where the new covers yet builds on the

old, is a powerful image and metaphor for the richness and diversity of feminist visionary thought, art, music, spirituality, and political action. Weaving images abound in feminist literature and women's cultural expressions. However, it is not enough simply to affirm weaving as a visionary image. To deepen and broaden our understanding of weaving, I want to show how weaving has become, and continues to become, a kind of contemporary feminist praxis. To see weaving as a way of reflecting upon the realities of the world and acting faithfully within it informs women's preaching at all levels. The content of preaching from a feminist perspective needs to reflect a vision of wholeness, a tapestry of human complexity and diversity. The prophetic edge of this kind of preaching calls the Christian community to integrative, weaving action in the world.

Specific Strands of Weft-faced Preaching

The strands of this vision of weaving the weft are many. I focus here on three of them: (1) feminist clarity and conviction that there is an interwoven, an interconnected, quality to all forms of oppression (i.e., sexism, racism, classism, ageism, militarism, heterosexism, and the oppression of lack of access); (2) feminist commitments to peace and disarmament and a vision about living in harmony with all creation; and (3) new feminist understandings of spirituality. Each of these strands of the weft reflects commitments rooted in values and ethics of solidarity, nonviolence, critical self-reflection, and a spirituality that is inseparable from one's work for social and political transformation.

One of the many strengths of feminist theologizing is that it makes no apology for starting the work of action and reflection with the concrete, real experience of women. Feminist theologizing does not begin with abstract concepts, strict models of understanding, or intellectual constructs. This chapter will mirror the process of feminist theologizing, for I begin the discussion about the vision of preaching from a feminist perspective by looking at the concrete experiences of women embodying feminist vision and move from there to suggest its implications for prophetic preaching. Feminist vision is illuminated by the lives of women themselves.

A book which documents the values and visions of one thousand North American women is entitled *This Way Daybreak Comes,* by Annie Cheatham and Mary Clare Powell. Their work attempts to give concrete expression to the many voices and faces of women's transforming vision within the United States and Canada. The intent is to demonstrate beyond doubt that women are in fact making a great impact on the world in which we live. They are creating and embodying new ways of relating to the earth, to other members of the human family, and to all creation. They are waging peace in creative and life-giving ways. They are confronting injustices of every nature and description. And they are healing wounds that continue to be an ongoing repercussion of a patriarchal, hierarchical worldview.

> Women are creating a new society. We are using intellect, intuition, politics, magic, and art to restructure existing institutions and invent new ones. . . . We do not mean that all women share the same mind, heart, culture, history, or vision. . . . On the contrary, we celebrate the diversity of women's paths. But we acknowledge the oneness of womankind, not only in our common oppression, but in our yearning for life.[7]

Aware of the many distinctions and differences among women, Cheatham and Powell still affirm that women offer transforming strands of vision and new life to our world. These strands of vision are articulated and lived out in the individual and collective lives of women everywhere around the globe. Their book portrays countless ordinary women doing extraordinary work in behalf of peace and justice, persisting in their efforts toward radical change.

> First, *women take the "self" as their major reference point.* Everywhere, they are questioning authority—of governments and social service agencies failing to serve; of religions and holy books that demean women; of the customs, mores, practices, and assumptions about women in a miso-

gynic culture. The second assumption builds on the first: *the "self" is the major reference point only in a context of connectedness.* . . . They want planetary resources to be shared; they respect ecological interdependence; they know that what happens to one affects all.[8]

The First Strand:
The Interwoven Quality of All Forms of Oppression

Few women travel thirty thousand miles to interview and talk with a thousand women about their visions and values, but many women continually experience the profound witness of other women's commitments to life, justice, and an integrated understanding of one's spiritual life with one's action in the world. There is one such experience from my own life of witnessing the visionary commitments and power of women globally that I now highlight as illustrative of the prophetic vision of women that is operative in our world today and influential directly and indirectly on preaching.

Nairobi, Kenya—Decade of Women Conference. In July 1985 I traveled with four women to Nairobi, Kenya, in order to participate in a nongovernmental forum connected with the official United Nations Conference celebrating the Decade of Women. The planners of the nongovernmental forum had anticipated as many as eight thousand women, but thirteen thousand attended. Women came from all parts of the world and represented thousands of organizations, institutions, and personal interests and commitments. They came not because they had an official vote at the United Nations Conference. They came not because their expenses were paid so as to make it possible and convenient to attend. They came because they were committed to dialogue, feminist strategizing and networking, and change in the world. They came to listen, to share, to plan for the future, and to take action. There were well over a thousand workshops, an unknown number of informal, spontaneous gatherings birthed by common interests and work, and countless opportunities to study and learn in Kenya.

One particular workshop had a profound impact on me as a

white, middle-class, Western woman. It was a three-hour workshop on global feminism. It was heartening to hear women from all over the world embrace feminism as a radical critique of all present systems of domination and oppression. In this context, feminism was not trivialized as a "white, middle-class, Western woman's issue," although I can appreciate this valid critique. The transforming quality of the workshop for me was the fact that for three hours not one single woman from the United States spoke. There were many places in the forum and many workshops where it was abundantly clear that white, Western women must listen in ways that are long overdue. It was not a passive, uninvolved listening; rather it was an act of justice and solidarity with women whose voices have too long been silenced. The commitment to hear other women's reality was paramount at the forum. In this workshop alone there were translators for eight different languages. As I sat and listened, and as I moved through those days of transformation, I was continually aware that the sharing and embodying of visions demand intense hard work, perseverance, and expense at all levels of women's lives. Yet this is exactly what women appear to be willing to invest in order to bring their transforming visions into reality. The Nairobi forum made clear for me in a new way the reality of the first aspect of feminist vision: All oppressions—all our lives—are interwoven connections.

All Oppressions—All Our Lives— ## Are Interwoven Connections

The visions that women hold for the present and for the future are diverse and multifaceted tapestries of longings and hopes. Yet I am amazed at one significant similarity. Almost all feminist writers, artists, and activists speak about *connections*— the interwoven quality of life, the webs of our relatedness, the interrelatedness of issues of oppression and justice, and the particularity of differences. Voices from the Christian church and the larger feminist community in the United States surround us continually with visions of the woven quality of our struggles for justice and transformation. I share these words, though lengthy, for the diversity of women's voices needs to be heard:

As we think about the future and about spirituality and about envisioning, I really see the importance of people's understanding their connection to one another. What women are about is this whole thing of connections—building them, maintaining them, nurturing them, and having them as part of their lives. It is this kind of practice that must be esteemed in a feminist world, that must be at the forefront of a feminist world.[9]

My hope springs from a strong belief that all creation is very much intertwined, that all life is sacred. Our various colors, cultures, and languages would co-exist without one group assuming a moral imperative to dominate. A feminist world would mean that all but the poorest of us Americans would be uncomfortable, that our assumptions would be shaken and that a drastic redistribution of resources would occur.[10]

Just as the patriarchal culture has been created from man's experience, or more precisely, from white middle-and-upper class man's experience, feminists are creating a new world culture based upon women's experience. Just as patriarchal culture has been built upon beliefs of separateness, hierarchy, and mechanism, feminists are building a new culture based upon beliefs of interconnectedness and integrity of all life forms.[11]

Feminist ethicists could generate action that mediates and heals the conflicts emerging as Anglo-American and Afro-American women struggle together for empowerment—when they each hold on to traditional supportive alliances from their past while trying *together* to create new relational forms of independence in the present. . . . Both need an ethic built upon moral, spiritual, and aesthetic principles redefined to be in deadly conflict with notions of good, beauty, God, right and wrong based on white supremacy and male superiority.[12]

The first strand of the weft of transforming feminist vision is the clear affirmation that all structures of oppression are interconnected and related. Within the feminist movement, historically and at present, this visionary understanding is missing in its fullest radicality. A growing number of women, speaking from a wide range of cultural, political, and social situations, continue to be committed to a feminist vision that seeks to take seriously every form of oppression affecting women's lives and listens carefully to the particularities of differing world realities. The ever-growing number of feminist writers, writing from the perspectives of race, age, differently abled situations, religious and spiritual diversity, suggests the persistent expansion of feminist visionary work.

The First Strand Grows Clearer

Barbara Smith, in *Home Girls: A Black Feminist Anthology,* addresses the myths that Black women have been encouraged to believe about the feminist movement and its issues. I lift up one for consideration: Myth 4: "Women's issues are narrow, apolitical concerns. People of color need to deal with the larger struggle."[13] In her response to this myth, Smith highlights the connections that feminism makes concerning the relatedness of issues of oppression and suggests the breadth of its vision in these words: "I have often wished I could spread the word that a movement committed to fighting sexual, racial, economic, and heterosexist oppression, not to mention one which opposes imperialism, anti-Semitism, the oppressions visited upon the physically disabled, the old and the young, at the same time that it challenges militarism and imminent nuclear destruction is the very opposite of narrow."[14] The challenge of the book stretches into every corner of feminist thought and work, and leaves all women and men realizing we have a long way to go before our transforming vision will ever become reality. As a Black woman, she confronts white women with their own persistent racism and confronts her Black sisters with their sexism. As a Black lesbian, she confronts with stinging clarity the oppressive structures and attitudes of heterosexism.

In her poem "Who Said It Was Simple?" Audre Lorde points to those who would not see the connection between race and sex:

There are so many roots to the tree of anger
that sometimes the branches shatter
before they bear.

Sitting in Nedicks
the women rally before they march
discussing the problematic girls
they hire to make them free.
An almost white counterman passes
a waiting brother to serve them first
and the ladies neither notice nor reject
the slighter pleasures of their slavery.
But I who am bound by my mirror
as well as my bed
see in color
as well as sex

and sit here wondering
which me will survive
all these liberations.[15]

It is not just Afro-American women who confront and expand feminist vision to include the realities of women of color.
Latina, Asian American, Native American women of diverse
tribal backgrounds, and Hispanic women are also redefining
feminism in radically diverse ways. A monumental book in its
time, *This Bridge Called My Back: Writings by Radical Women
of Color* was published originally in 1981 and became one of the
first resources to give voice to the diversity of women's voices,
oppressions, and world perspectives.[16] It remains a critical book
toward building a more inclusive, interwoven vision of justice
and human wholeness.

Within the context of the Christian church and, more
specifically, Christian feminism, Beverly Harrison as a Christian
ethicist and Isabel Carter Heyward as a Christian theologian
have confronted those of us who are white, middle-class women
of Christian heritage to push our connections deeper and wider.
Heyward, in *Our Passion for Justice,* and Harrison, in *Making
the Connections,* ask all women to look at the basis for their
ethical decisions and actions in the world and the religious and
theological underpinnings of their praxis.[17] Their contributions
to Christian feminist vision, in relation to a clear recognition

that all issues of oppression are interwoven and connected, are invaluable.

> Genuine solidarity involves *not mere* subjective identification with oppressed people but concrete answerability to them. Solidarity is accountability, and accountability means being vulnerable, capable of being changed by the oppressed, welcoming their capacity to critique and alter our reality. . . . A theology of liberation must be capable of an analysis that clarifies how oppression is interstructured.[18]

Harrison's perceptive insights enable her throughout the book simultaneously to offer sharp critiques of traditional Christian ethical thought and practice, and concrete visionary hope. With relational connectedness as her moral and ethical imperative, she seeks to demonstrate the connections between sexuality, morality and procreative choice, misogyny and homophobia, the disempowerment of aging adults, the conservation and redistribution of energy resources, and many additional pertinent issues linked to our work for justice. The weft of her feminist Christian vision is complex and tightly woven.

Heyward charts for us by way of sermons, speeches, prayers, and poetry, the movement of one Christian feminist in her struggle and movement toward clarity of vision. Her writing embodies a dynamic and growing awareness of the interconnectedness of issues of oppression. She clearly suggests that feminist theology has little to do with self-fulfillment but rather is grounded in a heightened sense of connection and relation. It is collective and communal.[19]

> Love is concrete—a matter of feeding and being fed; of touching and being touched; of making justice in the world. . . . I do not envision our goal as "oneness" or "sameness" but rather as right-relation, an operative sisterly bonding marked by mutual respect, trust, and advocacy that can be built over time in shared realization that this right relation is key to our survival.[20]

Regardless of whether one looks to the wisdom and insight of feminist theologians within the Christian church or seeks the perceptions of feminist theory rooted in political and social analysis that is found in voices from women outside any institutional religious structure, the feminist message in terms of overarching vision is closely related and surprisingly similar. The transforming vision of feminism today certainly involves the growing awareness that all the issues affecting women's lives are issues of importance and are ultimately interrelated. As feminism develops its radical critique of all systems of domination and oppression, the vision expands to include more and more women's voices.

Missing Strands

As I reflect on this wealth of feminist research and theology, I grow increasingly aware of two areas related to women's lives which need serious attention. These two areas have to do with women and aging, and women who are differently abled. Even though in recent years there has been an increase of resources concerning these issues, there still are not enough. I am very aware also that women who preach in many mainline denominations will encounter these issues frequently in parish ministry, in spite of the invisibility of the oppression.

It ought to be clear to many people in this country that ageism, the systematic oppression of older adults, is a reality. Older people are disenfranchised at so many levels of their existence. Recent statistics about the growing number of women and children who are in poverty also reveal the economic oppression of a larger number of older women. A transforming feminist vision must pay particular attention to the needs of older women and the injustices they face, as well as address the entire issue of ageism in our culture.

> The sources of alienation and dehumanization operating on the lives of those who are older are political, economic, and cultural, not merely symbolic or psychological. . . . Older persons do need to hear the call of others to struggle to express their power, their creativity, their ongoing strength to live fully as God's people.[21]

Feminist visionary work and thought needs to take into account the link between sexism, racism, classism, and ageism. The same system that creates and perpetuates oppressive structures and attitudes about sex, class, and race also has created structures and prejudices against older people in our society.

Perhaps a form of oppression that is even more invisible than the plight of the older person is the plight of the person who is differently abled. Only recently have women within the feminist movement begun to write and speak honestly about their silent and pervasive experiences of oppression. The feminist community has, for about ten years, been aware of the deaf community. Almost all of the concerts featuring women's music that I have attended in the past ten years have had sign language interpreters. Long before this was an issue of major significance to others, long before there was much public awareness, many feminist women musicians attempted to address the exclusion of the hearing impaired. There is still much to be done and much awareness to be woven into feminist vision about the connections between oppression of those who are differently abled and those who suffer other forms of injustice and oppression.

In response to terminology, Yvonne Duffy, in ... *All Things Are Possible,* speaks about her appreciation of a collective of women who first began to use the term *differently abled.*

> Differently Abled! What a wonderful phrase to describe those of us who, because of physical limitations, have learned so many other ways of carrying out everyday activities! To a woman who, for so long, has been denied by society any legitimacy in these areas, this is a heady term indeed, one that has changed my whole way of looking at myself. I am much indebted to the We Want the Music Collective and the Tucson, Arizona, lesbian community who originally coined it.[22]

It was particularly exciting for me to read Duffy's acknowledgment, for the collective of women she speaks about are the women who sponsor the Michigan Womyn's Music Festival each year. This is a musical and cultural event attended by several thousand women from all over the United States and other countries. The term *differently abled* appears in all their publicity. But this is only the beginning of the collective's commitment to differently abled women and their concerns and needs. At the festival itself (which takes place on a large space of very rugged land in Michigan), women construct ramps for wheelchairs, build special showers, have a sign language interpreter for each concert in the afternoon and evening, and invite participants to spend some amount of time with a woman who might need special assistance as a part of one's personal and collective contribution toward the "smooth running" of the festival. I have experienced this festival two times in my life, and both times I was overwhelmed by the radical inclusiveness. I have not witnessed this level of inclusiveness anywhere else in my life, certainly not in most of our religious institutions and churches. This annual event has broadened the consciousness of thousands of women, particularly in the area of the needs and concerns of differently abled women. This festival has broadened the very shape of feminist vision.

In a collection entitled *With the Power of Each Breath: A Disabled Women's Anthology,* edited by Susan E. Browne, Debra Connors, and Nanci Stern, fifty-four women speak about their anger, their growing awareness of their own oppression, and sources for coping. In addition to raising consciousness about the breadth of situations that face differently abled women, it also confronts our society with the need for profound structural and systematic changes:

> The needs and capabilities of disabled women are not taken seriously because of our gender as well as our physical or emotional differences. . . . Accessibility is the common denominator of disabled women's demands. We are disabled more by barriers of access than from the specific conditions of our bodies. . . . By accessibility we mean access to the same choices accorded able-bodied people. . . . A radical change in perspective is needed.[23]

Just as the entire system benefits from greater accessibility, the entire system also must be held accountable for perpetuating a situation that keeps differently abled persons invisible and excluded. An increasing number of women see the distinctive needs and vision of differently abled people as central to an expanding feminist vision.

Some of the women who are providing leadership in helping all women make connections between the lives and faith realities of differently abled women and women who are temporarily "abled bodied" are women within the Christian church. A United Methodist woman pastor, Kathy Black, who has served a deaf congregation in Maryland, describes the ministry of her congregation and her own pastoral ministry. When she preached she always used a combination of spoken word and sign language. I asked her what her motivations were to become involved and committed to deaf ministry. Her reply was, "It was a simple matter of inclusiveness."[24] To change the structures that need to be changed in order to alleviate suffering and oppression in the lives of differently abled people is not this simple; yet perhaps the essence of the vision is indeed that simple, and the connections continue. Three personal friends in San Francisco—Holly; Elizabeth, and Laurel, all United Methodist laywomen—have raised my consciousness as a woman in ministry as well as the consciousness of an entire congregation regarding the special gifts and needs of the deaf community. All their worship services are interpreted by a sign language interpreter, and out of that congregation a deaf choir was born—all living symbols, embodiments, of an inclusive vision.

One of my critiques of Christian feminist theology is that it has not taken seriously enough the needs, issues, and gifts of differently abled women, men, and children. There is a glaring void in the literature concerning this part of our vision. Perhaps some of the visionary leadership concerning this issue is coming from Christian churches because it is in this context that the need is felt and experienced so poignantly. I hope this issue will continue to be addressed in the future work and writings of feminist theologians and in the praxis of feminist pastors and preachers.

Judy Small, an Australian musician, sings a song called "Speaking Hands and Hearing Eyes" in an attempt to broaden our commitments and our awareness of differently abled people:

Jeffrey is just six years old, the biggest smile you ever
saw and there's so much I know he wants to say.
But Jeffrey cannot speak to me in language I can understand.
But oh the thoughts his fingers can convey.

So I'm learning to speak with my hands
I'm learning how to hear with my eyes
So that I can understand what he wants to say to me.

Sarah is my mother's age, the dignity shines from her face
There's much about her life I'd like to learn.
She tries to read my lips, but I can see frustration in her eyes,
And most of what she says I can't discern.

So I'm learning to speak with my hands
I'm learning how to hear with my eyes
So that I can understand what she wants to say to me.

I know she can't do it all my way
But if I meet her half way
There's no telling what good friends she and I could be.

No cane in your hand, no chair identifies you.
Silent and invisible your lives
So much to offer and our hearing world denies you
Seeing only handicapped in the language of your signs.

So I'm learning to speak with my hands
I'm learning how to hear with my eyes
So that I can understand what you want to say to me.

I know we can't do it all my way
But if I meet you half way
There's no telling what good friends you and I could be.
There's no telling what good friends you and I could be.[25]

The feminist vision of discerning, clarifying, and articulating
the interconnections of issues of oppression and injustice calls
for affirming the great human diversity among us. This act of
affirmation is profoundly dependent on our being open enough
to receive the giftedness of difference and courageous enough to
alter our worldview. This vision is dependent on all of us tasting,
listening, hearing, touching, and feeling the life and faith realities of those with radically different life experiences and perspectives. Sharon D. Welch says, "I find in the women's movement

acceptance of the new, the unique, the nonuniversal. I find in sisterhood a commitment to liberation and an openness to different ways of understanding and reaching liberation. . . . Universal discourse is the discourse of the privileged."[26] Universal discourse, or a failure to acknowledge human diversity, is an act not only of privilege but also of oppression.

Preachers Discerning This New Weft Strand

When we look at the connection between this first strand of the weft and women's preaching, the most profound homiletical response might be radical listening and discerning. Even though most homiletics literature does not reflect new visionary thought about what it means to be prophetic in preaching, many scholars and preachers continue to recognize the crucial role of listening in the total ministry of the preacher and pastor. If preachers are ever to grasp the feminist vision of interconnectedness, there must be much listening done before one even attempts to preach. Not only do preachers need to listen to the diverse voices within the Christian communities in which they speak, but they must also listen to those who are outside those communities.

We must listen to people when they come to worship, and we must bring to that context our common humanity. Proclamation is the task of the community, not merely of an individual.[27] Many preachers have not taken seriously enough the mandate to listen to the community and to approach the task and craft of preaching as a communal and collective act. I would be bold enough to suggest that preachers who preach out of a feminist perspective often see the preaching task and craft as a collective and shared responsibility. Their capacity to view and experience preaching in such a communal way has been aided by the interconnected vision that I have been illuminating. Until all preachers are willing to open themselves to the voices in their communities and to be changed by those voices and insights, the preaching act will remain individualistic in nature, and the content of sermons will be less than inclusive, isolated from the needs and wisdom of the whole people of God.

Fred Craddock, in his book *Overhearing the Gospel,* writes

about the act of listening in relation to preaching. He wonders what factor keeps people from listening the most and suggests "the dead air of familiarity," where too much is known and not enough is surprise. How do you enable a *new* hearing?[28] Even though Craddock is speaking about the reasons people do not listen to sermons, I believe that his question applies to the act of listening and opening oneself to another person in general. While I agree that people are not listening to sermons or to each other, I would add a harsher critique: The content of preaching is not prophetic enough, nor is it relevant to many of the issues I have attempted to name throughout this chapter. Much of the preaching that takes place in mainline Protestant churches does not stretch people to make connections between themselves and others or between the issues they face in their everyday lives and the larger political, social, and cultural realities of our world.

On the other hand, I also know that when preachers do listen and do challenge congregations to make those difficult connections, people still do not listen. Some sermons are too prophetic and too radical. These prophetic sermons, urging people to make the hard connections, are particularly difficult for people to hear when they are spoken by feminist women. Although there are not enough of these sermons, at the same time I am aware that when they are preached there is much resistance and denial. There are many reasons people do not listen. It may be that our language and message is not relevant or some of our sermons are much too prophetic in their visionary message and confrontation. Nevertheless, I am suggesting that for preaching to be prophetic today, all preachers might listen more to the multitude of voices and life perspectives within their communities of faith, might be guided by a feminist vision that all things are connected and interwoven.

I conclude this section about the first strand of the weft with the words from a song. While writing this section, I received a tape of women's music, written and sung by clergywomen in the Baltimore Annual Conference of the United Methodist Church and dedicated to "all the silent (silenced) ones: racial ethnics, lesbians, third world, other-abled." The songs speak of a feminist vision for our ministry, for our preaching. Clarifying the interrelatedness among us and giving it a voice might also be understood as "making room for the silences."

> So many voices singin', so many songs to sing,
> Don't overlook the silences
> That's where God's voice rings.
>
> Openin' up the spaces makin' room for the silences
> Hearin' the pain that never ever leaves your throat
> Sittin' down and listening long enough
> Outstretched arms and no one singin' a note.
>
> So many voices singin', so many songs to sing,
> Don't overlook the silences
> That's where God's voice rings.
>
> Openin' up the spaces makin' room for the silences
> Listenin' with passion to those who've never had a voice,
> Quieting the babble of our own fool tongues
> God's revelation is found in the silent ones.
>
> So many voices singin', so many songs to sing,
> Don't overlook the silences
> That's where God's voice rings.[29]

The Second Strand: Commitment to Peace, Nonviolence, Living in Harmony with All Creation

Central to feminist vision is peaceful existence, nuclear disarmament, and living in ecological and relational harmony with creation. Women, who know from their experience what it means to bring life into being, have passionate convictions about the protection and maintenance of life.

Greenham Common Women's Peace Camp. Just as the Nairobi conference was an embodiment of the feminist vision of the interconnections of women's lives, their differences, and the diversity of their oppressions, Greenham Common Women's Peace Camp is an embodiment of women's commitment to peace and nonviolence. I visited the camp in January 1986.

In August 1981 a small group of women organized a peace
march from Cardiff (South Wales) to Greenham Common,
a virtually unknown U.S. Air Force Base in England, 125
miles away, as a protest against the N.A.T.O. decision to
site 96 U.S. cruise missiles there. They arrived at the main
gate of the base on September 5th. Some decided to stay.
Others had to go home, but more women came, doubtless
never imagining that what quickly came to be called the
Greenham Common Women's Peace Camp would still be
there over four years later.[30]

It has now been many years later, and the peace camp is alive
and well. I visited there in January 1986 in order to support the
women who were there and educate myself about their global
witness for peace. It was a painful visit. The women were located
around the nine-mile perimeter. A group of women were living
and witnessing for peace at each of the seven gates.

I visited only one gate and interacted with approximately
eight women during my visit. The living conditions of the
women were beyond belief. It was wintertime, spitting snow and
very cold. The group of women at the yellow gate, or the main
gate, were huddled around a small fire. There were no tents in
which to sleep, no permanent shelters of any kind. Food and
simple belongings were stored in a van. A friend and I asked
what we could do to support their efforts. Quickly we were told
their needs—firewood and food. We left to obtain some of both
and returned. During the two hours we were there, the official
bailiffs came three times and forced the women to move from
their space, putting the fire out and forcing them to begin to
move down the road. It was obviously a game of control and
power.

These evictions often take place many times a day, always
several times a week. The bailiffs leave; and the women, representing a constant protest against cruise missiles and war, return
to huddle around the fire. They intend to stay until the missiles
are gone. Thousands of women have come to Greenham during
the years of the peace camp. At two different times, between
thirty and forty thousand women have gathered there, surrounding the entire perimeter with a circle for peace.[31]

Greenham is one of the most exciting political developments in recent years, completely outside party politics. It offers a challenge to left wing politic, with its male-dominated agendas and hierarchical style, and to the British peace movement which narrowly defines "peace" as disarmament. . . . Women have brought to a practice of nonviolence a challenging assertiveness, expressing themselves unequivocally in confronting the police and the military, and keeping that challenge alive, oppositional, and uncoopted.[32]

The women at Greenham Common Peace Camp give witness to a definition of peace that encompasses all of life. The missiles are the primary symbol of their resistance, but their vision is broad and inclusive. Peace is not just an issue for feminists such as these; it is a radically transforming vision. The power of their witness was overwhelming to me. Those fifty to seventy-five women (and this number changes throughout the year) who live there twenty-four hours a day, 365 days a year, provide a global witness for feminism and nonviolence.

For the past decade, Holly Near, a feminist musician and activist, has woven messages of nonviolence, concern for the earth, antinuclear politics, and relational harmony throughout most of her music. Her music has been central to feminist vision. In an album created with Ronnie Gilbert she sings about peace:

Ancient eyes are watching in the night
A star comes out to guide the way
The sun still shines despite the clouds
And the dawn is dusk is dawn is dusk is day
Farmers dream to rise and feed the world
The world awakes to feed the heart
Heart beats while a thousand flags are waving
And the farmers see a dream has played a part.

We will have peace, we will because we must
We must because we cherish life
And believe it or not, as daring as it may seem
It is not an empty dream, to walk in a powerful path
Neither the first nor the last in the great peace march
Life is a great and mighty march
Forever, for love and for life on the great peace march.

Black like night and red like clay
Gold like sun and brown like earth
Gray like mist and white like moon
My love for you, the reason for my birth
Peace can start to move in just one heart
From a small step to leaps and bounds
A walk becomes a race for time
And a brave child calls out to the crowd.

We will have peace, we will because we must
We must because we cherish life
And believe it or not, as daring as it may seem
It is not an empty dream, to walk in a powerful path
Neither the first nor the last in the great peace march
Life is a great and mighty march
Forever, for love and for life on the great peace march.[33]

Intertwined with a feminist vision of peace, nonviolence, and disarmament is a profound appreciation for life. This dimension of the vision gives it the breadth to encompass all of life. We must have peace because "we cherish life." "Human life must be first; all else second,"[34] "Ecological perspective is a basepoint of feminist theory."[35] For many feminist women, valuing life means there is no separation between ecological responsiveness, antinuclear political action, and protests against invasions of Central America. All these realities are interwoven and must be understood together. If feminist vision maintains that life is of utmost value, then all realities that diminish life must be confronted.

Dorothee Sölle, Christian theologian and activist, has written about the broad dimensions of peace and human wholeness in many of her books. Her work also involves severe critiques of those structures, institutions, and religious values that perpetuate violence and alienation. In *Choosing Life,* she describes consumer culture and its avoidance of suffering and struggle which, she says, is a denial of death. "To avoid suffering has advanced to the position of a major strategy in the consumer culture, whether physically by means of pills, psychologically by means of diversion, or politically through blindness. We have developed techniques of all kinds in order to avoid suffering, but what we are really avoiding is life itself."[36] Sölle is not romanticizing suffering; she is simply confronting her readers with the reality that suffering always accompanies our struggles for life. In another of her books, *Of War and Love,* Sölle has much to say about peace and life in relation to resistance and revolution:

> It means being at one with the power of life. It means feeling within ourselves the same power to heal and create, and to act on that power. It means organizing resistance against death. . . . Faith and struggle are one.[37]

Although there are those who might argue that pacifism is not an act of privilege, Sölle reminds us that countless strategies are needed to bring about justice and ultimate peace. Feminists are not in harmony about the diversity of strategies waged in the name of peace and life, yet the commitment to stand for life is central to feminist theology and spirituality.

One of the feminist books of our time that creatively explores, through the voices and experiences of many women, the connections between feminism and nonviolence is *Reweaving the Web of Life: Feminism and Nonviolence.* This book has helped to shape feminist vision in relation to issues of peace and justice.

> While the feminist movement has not overtly defined itself as nonviolent, by opposing oppressive institutions of domination, by employing nonviolent tactics, by pioneering in nonhierarchical structures, by formulating principles and identifying visions of harmony and liberation, it has become, I believe, the most powerful force for nonviolent revolution in practice.[38]

There is a strong alliance between the peace movement and the woman's movement, between nonviolence and feminism. The weaving together of these strands of our weft of visionary thought and action, however, demands that no strategies for peace will be complete without clear feminist analysis, and no feminist thought is adequate without strategies for peace and nonviolence.

If we look at this second strand of the weft and preaching, we see clear implications for the theology of what we proclaim. Claiming such a vision of peace, nonviolence, and an appreciation for life does not demand a theology that calls for sacrifice and suffering as goals in themselves. To be sure, suffering is a part of life, and often it is the price those who are committed to justice will pay. When the world is threatened with nuclear holocaust, the Christian church and those who bear witness to its message by word and action must speak and live for life, refusing to idolize death and suffering. Beverly Harrison confronts:

> It is one thing to live out a commitment to mutuality and reciprocity as the way to bear up God in the world and to be clear-eyed and realistic about what the consequences of that radical love may be. To be sure, Jesus was faithful unto death. He stayed with his cause and he died for it. He accepted sacrifice. But his sacrifice was for the cause of radical love, to make relationship and to sustain it, and above all, to righting wrong relationship, which is what we call "doing justice."[39]

The Third Strand: Feminist Spirituality

Woven throughout this chapter have been a number of insights and understandings that undergird feminist vision and spirituality. Before ending this chapter on the weft of feminist vision, however, I will reflect on three aspects particularly distinctive to feminist spirituality: (1) the inseparable link between political action, social transformation, and one's self-conscious spiritual life; (2) the affirmation and celebration of the human body as the locus for our movement and action in the world; and (3) a profound appreciation for diverse spiritual disciplines, perspectives, and practices as they contribute to an attempt to integrate a diversity of women's spiritual expressions and experiences within an understanding of feminist spirituality.

I begin my reflections on feminist spirituality once again with an experience from my own life, one that highlights the interwoven quality of the three dimensions just mentioned.

Women's Ritual Group. For a full year in Berkeley, California, from September 1985 to July 1986, I participated in a women's ritual group, meeting twice a month for nearly a year. All women in the group claimed explicit Christian roots and were involved in the institutional church. Four women were Roman Catholic women in community; three were Roman Catholic laywomen; and two were Protestant women, one an American Baptist laywoman and one a United Methodist clergywoman. Originally the group was created solely on the basis of mutual friendships and a certain degree of interest in participating in worship/ritual experiences that were explicitly feminist in content and process.

During the ten months that I was a part of the group, each woman took several turns facilitating the ritual experience. Even though all the women stand within the Christian tradition, the breadth of resources drawn upon were global, cross-cultural, and from a varied religious perspective. Aspects of Native American spirituality, Jewish spirituality, Goddess spirituality, and traditional Christian spirituality were interwoven throughout our worship/ritual expressions. More often than not there was dancing involved or other bodily movement in terms of touching, tasting, expressing with hands and whole bodies our responses to each other and the spirit. There was a clear understanding from the beginning that spirituality is not separate from our everyday lives nor isolated from our commitment to social justice and social transformation. This was my first experience of a sustained women's ritual group, committed to the balance between social transformation, spiritual contemplation and discipline, incarnational/bodily theologizing, and diverse/ global ritual expressions. It was powerful indeed and very empowering for each of our ministries in the larger world.

Spirituality and Social Transformation

Sharon Welch, in *Communities of Resistance and Solidarity,* speaks in a revolutionary way about the connections between spirituality and political and social transformation. "Liberating communities of faith show no separation between the spiritual and the political. . . . Spiritual transformation is inextricably tied to social and political transformation."[40] Though Welch speaks about all liberation movements and communities, this truth certainly is foundational to a feminist theology of liberation and to expressions of feminist spirituality. This truth must be repeated over and over, for we live in a time when the resurgence of interest in spirituality is quickly translated into notions of separateness from the world, denied bodily existence, and increased passivity. Such an understanding of spirituality is neither adequate nor appropriate in relation to feminist theology and spirituality.

Throughout her book, Welch continually stresses the essential and paramount place of resistance and action in the movement toward liberation and human wholeness. The measure of the faithfulness of any community will be evaluated on its capacity to bring about concrete changes in behalf of justice and its commitment to radical acts of transformation. I suggest that everything she says about the nature of Christian feminist theology and praxis might also be said about feminist spirituality. Christian feminists express and embody their spirituality with their concrete actions in the world for change and global justice. The two cannot be separated.

> The truth of God-language and of all theological claims is measured not by their correspondence to something eternal but by the *fulfillment of its claims in history, by the actual creation of communities of peace, justice, and equality.* The criterion of liberation faith and liberation theology is practice, or, more specifically, the process of liberation in history.[41]

Central to Welch's understanding of both liberation theology and feminist spirituality is her commitment to practice/ action and her equal commitment to remember suffering and oppression. What Welch is affirming, acts of remembering and acts of justice in the world, is exactly what I see operative in feminist spirituality. As I noted in Chapter 4, I see remembering/re-membering as central to the very experience of feminist women's experiences of community. And most Christian feminists realize that transforming action in the world is imperative.

Spirituality and Sacramental Embodiment

The second aspect of feminist spirituality that is crucial in a larger feminist vision is the absolute affirmation of bodily existence. This affirmation is in great contrast to countless expressions of traditional Christianity that deny the body and declare its expressions as evil. A growing awareness of the giftedness of our bodies is central to feminist spirituality. Perhaps it is because women's bodies in particular have been so abused and misused throughout human history that many women have become acutely aware of the importance of their body's full integration into any expression and understanding of spirituality. This affirmation of bodily existence has emerged within feminist thought and literature as a direct confrontation to traditional dualistic thinking still so prevalent in our modern world, i.e., the split between body and spirit, nature and history, feminine and masculine, and the rational and emotional. All of these dualisms are fundamentally in opposition to a feminist vision that sees all things as connected and interwoven. Isabel Carter Heyward affirms: "The characteristic that renders feminism unique among the various movements for human liberation is our emphasis on the body, woman's body in particular. . . . Theologically, our emphasis on body is a radically incarnational affirmation."[42] Feminism—and feminist spirituality—is indeed incarnational theology and practice.

The church's oppressive attitudes and moralizing regarding sexuality at all levels of human existence have emerged in part from a total denial of the body. Misogyny and homophobia have also been fueled by a denial of our bodies and a denial of sexual/sensual/relational expression. In harmony with the awareness that all things are connected and all forms of oppression are linked, a feminist spirituality must be grounded in an awareness of our integrated wholeness. Our bodies lead us to connect.[43] Also, I believe that many women have a keen awareness that there simply would be *no relation* without our embodied selves. It is not the worshiping of bodies that is at the heart of feminist spirituality; rather it is the vision of integration that continually seeks to bring together body, mind, and spirit.

Concerning feminist spirituality and its emphasis on bodily existence and the celebration of our women's bodies, I wish to reiterate that we have not heard enough from women who are differently abled and women who are aging. Feminist spirituality has yet to be fully influenced by the spiritual wisdom, insights, and practice of women who are distinctively challenged by their bodily existence. For preachers, this is clearly one of the important agendas of feminist spirituality to which we must attend as we learn and listen.

Diversity in Feminist Spirituality

The final aspect of feminist spirituality to be highlighted here pertains to the diversity of women's spiritual expressions and experiences. A particular strength of feminist spirituality is its capacity for diversity and difference. In order for our feminist vision to be broad and inclusive, feminist spirituality must also draw its life from a great variety of women's spiritual sources. It may be that this capacity for diversity in feminist spirituality has evolved because of a feminist commitment to the webs of interconnections and the giftedness of difference noted earlier in the chapter and because, for those of us who are Christian and feminist, there exists a growing awareness that the Christian tradition does not adequately represent the quality and essence of women's spiritual experience. It may be that many Christian feminists do not feel "bound" by traditional Christian spirituality both because it is not broad enough or inclusive enough in its vision and ritual expression and, even more, because it is fundamentally out of harmony with much of women's spiritual experience. Because traditional Christianity does not speak to many women's spiritual experience, it is absolutely necessary to move beyond the tradition to draw from a multitude of additional sources.

Spiritual Sources from Women's Culture

It is not that Christian feminists draw only from other explicitly religious sources in order to broaden and shape their spirituality. Rich sources from women's culture also inform and create new understandings of feminist spirituality. Many of these expressions are not explicitly "religious," yet they provide deepened understandings of the mystery of life and faith, a heightened awareness of global oppression and injustice, and a spirit of celebration that are essential to the weft of feminist spirituality.

One of the sources of feminist spirituality and vision that informs thousands of women today is "women's music." I have used here the words from several of the songs of feminist musicians. I have heard some of this music in conventional worship experiences in mainline Protestant churches and in Roman Catholic masses. I certainly have heard much of it used within women's gatherings, women's ritual groups, and countless religious and "secular" women's conferences. The power and message of women's music play a key role in the shape of feminist spirituality. Much of the power of women's music focuses around its celebrative spirit and its commitment to justice. It speaks about a wide range of human experience, often affirming realities in women's lives that are still silent and unacknowledged.

As with all art forms, women's music is also able to sing of women's oppression and suffering in such a way that women are empowered and inspired to be aware and to act in their own behalf and for the well-being of other women. Scarcely any theme of women's lives is left unexplored. Women's music pours forth confrontation about the physical abuse of women, the oppression of aging women, the economic exploitation of women of color, and the painful yearnings of women for a different way of life. Women's music also pours forth hopeful visions that cut across lines of race, class, and heterosexism; about powerful women in history and powerful women of today; about the distinctive love between two women; and the incredible sense of solidarity in sisterhood. Women's music is a moving force in women's culture and in feminist spirituality.

Countless clergywomen whom I have met have been influenced by the words, images, and celebrative spirit of women's music for at least the last decade. Some clergywomen, like the United Methodist clergywomen of the Baltimore Conference, have been inspired to write their own women's music after exposure to women's music in the larger context of the women's movement. For some clergywomen, the explicit integration of women's music into their sermons and worship experiences in local communities is still an impossible vision. For others, the gradual use of women's music has been possible, both in sermons and in worship celebrations. For all women who listen to women's music, I would boldly assert that it makes an enlarging, empowering impact on feminist spirituality and Christian feminist ministry.

As the reality of women's music has grown and "aged," it too has become increasingly inclusive in both the content of the lyrics and the growing number of women musicians who are women of color. This growth has only expanded and deepened the feminist vision expressed. Not only does a group like Sweet Honey in the Rock[44] embody confrontation and vision concerning Afro-American women in the United States, but they sing of African roots and spiritual wisdom as well. An artist like Holly Near[45] pushes to make connections between U.S. policies in Latin America, potential nuclear annihilation, the systematic oppression of gay and lesbian people, and the all-pervasive oppression of women of all classes, races, and cultural and social situations. Her music is like an interwoven tapestry of issues and convictions.

Feminist women's poetry and visual art have also contributed much to a growing feminist vision and a deeper spirituality. Both expressions begin with women's experience and then express, through words, forms, colors, and images, the "unnameable" mystery of women's lives. Whether it is the concrete reality of Judy Chicago's *Birth Project,*[46] the confrontation of Donna Kate Rushin's "Bridge Poem,"[47] or the vision of Adrienne Rich's *Dream of a Common Language,*[48] the celebration and affirmation of women's lives and women's truths are given expression in women's art. These expressions fundamentally make an impact on the nature and content of feminist vision and feminist spirituality. Women's artistic expressions continue to enable feminists to link spirituality with the everyday reality and experiences of diverse women.

There are a large number of Christian feminists who are

committed to weaving together sources from Christianity, sources from the larger women's community, and sources from within their own lives. The integration of this multitude of sources is central to the richness and the diversity that is the heart of feminist spirituality. We are weaving these strands of feminist spirituality into the larger weft of vision.

Feminist Vision—The Weft of Preaching

The feminist vision I have described and documented in many women's lives has varied implications for preaching from a feminist perspective. This vision becomes the weft of proclamation. The shape, color, texture, width, and pattern of weave will vary with the weft of each one who preaches. Even in the midst of different wefts that preachers weave, feminist vision does seem to reflect some common concerns and commitments. I have attempted to affirm and celebrate three of those common "weft threads": (1) the interwoven reality of the many experiences of oppression that women and other marginalized people face and the growing awareness of the giftedness of difference; (2) the deep commitment women have to living in harmony with life, to nonviolence, and to peace; and (3) the rich diversity of women's sources of truth, wisdom, images, and experiences from which women are shaping a feminist spirituality. Strands of these three aspects of women's commitments and women's experience appear to permeate most expressions of feminist vision.

For preachers, to choose the weft of feminist vision as an integral part of our proclamation creation is to choose to be involved in prophetic preaching, individually and collectively. It is clear to me that in a culture and society that does not value or embody much of what is at the heart of feminist vision, it is radical and reaffirming to preach with this vision ever before us. Many people in local Protestant congregations will meet this prophetic preaching with resistance and anger. There are others who will welcome it as incredibly hopeful and powerfully relevant. Transformation and change are always met with the entire range of human responses. This must not deter us from our commitments to a new kind of preaching.

I have outlined the nature and essence of the weft of feminist vision as I experience and understand it. It is a vision that judges, enlivens, and engenders hope. It is a vision of transformation and will reshape the world as we know it into something radically new.

6

Weave Variations:
Principles of Design

Therefore, for purposes of this discussion, design is defined as
the ordered arrangement of parts to make a whole. . . . Order*ed*
does not necessarily mean order*ly,* for a tangled mass of yarns
may in fact be planned and therefore designed.

It is impossible to make anything without designing it, either
consciously or unconsciously, for design implies a series of
choices: the choice of one yarn over another, the choice of one
color instead of a second, the choice of a particular size or
shape. The weaver's concern is not with designing *per se,* but
with creating an *effective* design—one that fulfills the requirements of the item to be woven and that simultaneously satisfies
the artist's aesthetic goals.[1]

As all weavers come to know, it is at this point in the process
that the greatest creativity and the greatest freedom is demanded of the weaver. The creative and adventurous weaver
will embrace this moment with enthusiasm, joy, and certainly
some healthy anxiety. The cautious weaver will be forever
trapped by the limitations of "tried and true" patterns and
designs. This is the moment that any true artist or craftsperson
waits for, the moment when all the necessary requirements are
in place and personal inspiration, style, and vision come soaring
forward.

Initially, as I was learning to weave, I did not realize what
freedom and creativity were ultimately demanded of the weaver.
Orienting one's self to the loom and all its capabilities, learning

the tedious and difficult task of placing the warp threads on it and choosing what color and texture the weft threads would be were all I imagined was involved. Very soon, however, one discerns that all of these steps are preliminary actions to creating the actual design one will weave into the cloth. The creation of that design is what distinguishes accomplished weavers from novices.

The same can and must be said about the preaching craft. One can do brilliant exegetical work, wrestle faithfully with how the ancient biblical text and the contemporary situation intersect, and polish one's speech and style of proclamation; yet, this is never enough. If the proclaimed word is not an art piece, woven together into a beautiful tapestry of meaning and power, each part interlaced with every other part, it is stripped of its beauty and transforming essence. When weaving possesses this interwoven quality it is the best that the craft can offer. When sermons are interwoven witnesses to the vision and radical power of the Christian faith in all its confrontation and hope, those proclaimed words are also the best the craft can offer.

I have suggested that preaching from a feminist perspective has at its heart this vision of interwoven power and truth. The intent is toward justice, wholeness, and hope. The commitment to work faithfully with the Christian tradition, i.e., God language, Christology, biblical authority, hermeneutics, and also issues of authority and intimacy, is fundamentally understood. The unrelenting conviction to move beyond the boundaries of the tradition toward a transforming vision is also a painful and uncompromising given. For feminist preachers, the intimate weaving of our lives with the lives of those who are in community with us is of paramount concern, and the nonauthoritarian empowerment of all is of ultimate value. As with the weaver, however, this is only the starting point. What each individual preacher ultimately does with these basic realities has to do with design and style.

Design Principles

The principles of design are guidelines to be considered in developing a design. . . . Whether a design "works" is a highly subjective and empirical judgment based partly on such nebulous concepts as taste and aesthetic sensibility, as well as long observation of designs that *do* work. . . . One speaks of a design as being *effective* or *successful,* and any design is so when it satisfies the artist's aesthetic impulse and communicates with the audience.[2]

The weaver creates an artistic creation with guiding principles of design and with imagination. The weaver takes seriously aesthetic sensitivities as well as the needs of those for whom the weaving is originally intended. A skilled artist knows when to use the principles of design to enhance and enliven the work, but also sees clearly the times when, in order to accomplish the finished product desired, one must depart from all traditional expectations of design. These delicate and difficult decisions are the part of any great artist's work. No less is true of the preacher and her or his craft.

In the few pages remaining, I will restate and summarize a few of the most important aspects of preaching from a feminist perspective. I am using the concept of design to organize and give further clarification to several strands of preaching already mentioned throughout this work.

There are many principles of design that might guide my remaining comments about the distinctive quality of feminist preaching, but I have chosen four. These four have a technical relationship to the craft of weaving itself and have poignant relevancy for the art of preaching. "There is little agreement about just how many design principles there are. . . . For purposes of this discussion, four seems an adequate and understandable number, those four being proportion, balance, emphasis, and rhythm."[3]

Proportion

Proportion refers to the relationships of size or other measurable quantity among the elements in a design or between an object and its environment.[4]

Throughout this exploration of preaching in a feminist perspective I have consistently asserted that the beginning point of research and insight needs always to begin with women themselves and their experienced reality.

In Chapter 1 I sought to make the connection between the image and metaphor of weaving as it is emerging in women's culture and life experience, and weaving as a visionary metaphor for preaching. I chose weaving initially because it appears so frequently in the stories, resources, and creations of *women's lives.*

In Chapter 2 I drew upon selected psychological and sociological research by women scholars. The intent of this chapter was to illumine how women might understand and create a sense of intimacy in their preaching in light of women's psychological, moral, and ethical development, and in light of particular structures of socialization. *Women's lives* were again the starting point.

In Chapter 3 the focus was on a feminist critique of authority and suggested new paradigms of understanding. These paradigms emerge from *women's lives.*

In Chapter 4 I focused on the critique of three aspects of the Christian tradition articulated and proclaimed by contemporary women scholars. This critique is both an individual and a collective prophetic movement in our time, seeking to transform the very shape and structures of the Christian church. The critique comes out of the midst of *women's lives:* their rage, marginality, constructive theologizing, and commitment to justice.

In Chapter 5 I documented women's experience of living and embodying feminist vision: at a global women's conference in Nairobi, at a missile base in England, and in the everyday lives of women ritualizing and celebrating new understandings of feminist spirituality. The living actualities of women's feminist witness in the world become the threads for the creation of a new vision and hope for the future of the human family. *Women's lives,* their struggles to address oppression, their faithful witness to peace and nonviolence, and their expanding threads of spirituality all weave together to create transformation.

Throughout this work, I have articulated this phenomenon of

beginning with *women's lives* as the source for wisdom, insight, and truth as *women's naming.*

> Women have called the process of giving form to their experience through words a *new naming.* . . . As women begin to name the world for themselves not only will they create new life possibilities for women, they will also upset the world order that has been taken for granted for centuries.[5]

This new naming is central to any feminist task and to the act of proclamation. Perhaps one of the reasons women are so excited about the craft and act of preaching has to do with naming. Until very recently in human history, women have been denied access to positions and places of naming. Women's deepest and most profound experiences of faith, of relationality, of God, and of incarnation have not been named. Preaching is a central place in the life of the Christian church where such naming can begin and where naming occurs. The new naming of women will broaden the Christian tradition, deepen the Christian faith, and widen the vision of Christian transformation. Women and other marginalized people take this responsibility very seriously, for we know from our own experience what it means to be excluded from the power and creativity of naming. Our lives have been so influenced by naming that is not our own that we are painfully aware of its incredible power and awesome potential to shape and create reality.

The choice to summarize and clarify women's naming under the first design principle of proportion is intentional. Because women's lives are not the beginning point of naming reality in so many places in our world, I choose to give ultimate valuing to the witness of our lives.

A word now of concern and caution about *proportion* must, however, be voiced. I am aware that the choice to begin research with the actual realities of women's lives is both a philosophical and theological decision. One could argue the dangers of narcissism and limited vision. One could argue the dangers of individualism and total subjectivity. These are legitimate concerns to raise, yet they are addressed, I would hope, by the very nature and design of the research. It is not the individual development of one woman that motivates women's psychology; rather it is the collective experience of female gender identity and development. It is not the individual critique of a single Christian feminist that creates feminist theology; it is the collective commitment of women to address marginality and injustice within the institution of the Christian church. It is not the individual witness of one feminist visionary that gives shape to feminist vision; it is the collective transforming action of women around the globe. An individual woman's life is forever viewed in relation to the larger reality of all women's lives. And thus, women's psychology, Christian feminist critique, and the visions of global feminism keep expanding.

The very nature of feminism is collective. At the same time, feminist insight, critique, and vision force us to take seriously the fullness of individual women's lives. This harmony between the individual and the collective is at the heart of women's naming process and is thus at the heart of feminist women's preaching. One woman's weaving ought never to be more important in *proportion* to the whole, nor should one woman's weaving ever be less important in *proportion* to the whole. The wholeness of our women's truth exists both in the individual and in the collective. Each part of the weaving design, each woven proclamation created depends on harmonious proportions of single strand and whole.

The harmony between the individual and the collective that is at the heart of feminism influences preaching in yet another important way. I believe this balance sensitizes women and men to other important issues of harmony and integration. This may be the reason feminist women are so committed to a nonauthoritarian style in their preaching, remembering that the voices of the community are of importance equal to the preacher's. Many feminist women are utterly convinced that the preaching craft is one collectively experienced in the Christian community. The preacher speaks on behalf of the community, never abdicating one's own voice but also never allowing one's own voice to dominate or silence others. Proportion in one's preaching design does not solely apply to the weaving itself, but also to how the weaving is done by all.

Balance

> Balance is the condition that exists when all forces are in
> a state of equilibrium. . . . After much experimentation the
> designer learns to sense when a composition is balanced.[6]

In preaching from a feminist perspective, the balance between
warp and weft must be noted. I have suggested that when
women and men preach from a feminist consciousness their
weaving proclamations are "weft-faced," more influenced by
transformation than by tradition. Yet there are key ways the
warp and weft actually work together.

As is obvious by now, the warp and weft are inextricably
interwoven. One can weave a creation that allows equal parts of
warp and weft to show as easily as one can weave a creation that
allows warp or weft to dominate. The final result is in the design,
the intention, and the desire of the weaver. It is absolutely clear
to all weavers, however, that without the warp, weaving cannot
take place. The warp is foundational for weaving. So it is with
feminist preaching. Feminist preachers from within the Christian tradition take a stand at countless places in it. Our critiques
range from moderate to radical, and our positions within the
institutional church range from center to margin. Regardless of
where we stand, our preaching builds from the tradition out.
For a "weft-faced" weaving, the warp strands must be particularly strong and durable. They do not need to be colorful or
aesthetically pleasing, but they must be durable.

The Christian tradition endures in feminist preaching, perhaps in remnants, perhaps in transformed language and images,
but it does endure. To preach without a strong commitment to
the tradition, even in the midst of transforming it, is to stand
rootless as a preacher. The collective joys, struggles, idolatries,
faithful stories, mistakes, and visions of the Christian community are interwoven throughout the tradition of our faith. The
contemporary community needs to know and have access to
those collective realities in order to shape lives of faith today.

The balance between warp and weft—critique and vision—is
a difficult one to maintain. I do not propose an easy solution.
I simply and profoundly believe that for the tradition to be
disengaged from its oppressive roots (if that is, in fact, even

possible), Christian feminist women who are preaching must do so from the vision of critique and possibility. The discerning preacher is never unaware, however, of the durable warp strands that give substance and shape to the weft strands that show forth.

Emphasis

Emphasis suggests that one particular part of a design catches and holds the viewer's eye more than any other. One's attention is directed—either gradually or immediately—to some focal point or points and is held there.[7]

Emphasis in the design is related to that which stands out, that which catches the eye, that which captures our attention and focuses our awareness. Emphasis in the craft of weaving can be created by any one of several elements: color, size, texture pattern of a particular weave, or contrasting shapes. It can be blatant or subtle, restful or compelling. The point of emphasis is always noticed by the way it contrasts with the rest of the weaving design.

Two elements of emphasis stand out in the design work of preaching from a feminist perspective. I have mentioned these two facets of preaching earlier in the work, but I wish to highlight them here in relation to the very distinctive design of proclamation. The first is the element of self-revelation, and the second is the element of image and imagination.

The two observations that were most widely made among the homiletics professors I interviewed were (1) women reveal much more of themselves in their preaching than do men, and (2) women tend to use the imagination more than do men. I will build on these observations of teachers in the field, for they made special note of these points of emphasis in the preaching of many women.

Self-revelation. In regard to women and self-revelation, even though most professors were clear that greater self-revelation occurred in women's preaching, none of them articulated why this was true. Let me suggest two reasons why women reveal much more of themselves in the preaching act, both reasons related to assertions articulated previously.

First, women see preaching fundamentally as a relational act. In Chapter 2 the research would suggest that women are socialized to be more relational and are more able to be vulnerable and self-revealing in general. This alone does not suggest mutuality or solidarity in the preaching act, which is the ultimate desire of relationships built from a feminist perspective. However, when a feminist consciousness is added to these insights about women's relational style, one moves in the direction of non-hierarchical, dialogical modes of relating and communicating. The combination of these two elements, relationality and a commitment to mutuality and solidarity, produces a preaching style that demands that the preacher be personally very present in the craft and act of proclamation. Relationships are built on the sharing of self with another; mutual relationships are created on the equity of all people having opportunity and responsibility for the sharing of self. Women committed to feminist understandings of mutuality and solidarity reveal more about themselves in the preaching act in order to establish, enhance, and deepen the relational power between themselves and the community. Preaching is not a time to distance one's self from the community; rather it is a time to enhance the relational life of the entire community by one's self-example.

Second, for women and men, preaching is an act of theologizing, and feminist theologizing always begins with one's own experience. Throughout the previous chapters I have suggested that the entry point of women into questions of authority, intimacy, critique, and vision is their own experience. This is a basic tenet of feminist theology. For women and men with a feminist consciousness, preaching is no exception to the processes and guidelines of theologizing from a feminist perspective. If this is a working assumption, one would necessarily weave throughout one's preaching many aspects of one's own life of faith. Feminist preachers who preach believe as feminist theologians do, that we must claim our own lives as rich resources for religious understandings, wisdom, and insight.

In a section of *God's Fierce Whimsy* entitled "The Language of Feminist Theology: Inclusive of Women's Experiences," the

Mud Flower Collective reflect on the transformation of language as women come into their own power and speech:

> To begin with the bits and pieces of our daily lives, striving
> for honesty and authentic speech, is to start with the power
> we have at hand. . . . Something new cannot be discovered,
> revealed, or offered unless the discoverer owns up to what
> difference this discovery or insight makes in her or his life.[8]

Unlike much traditional homiletical method, our lives are not
simply illustrative of the biblical text; rather our lives are a kind
of living text of God's revelation with a power and integrity all
its own. The biblical text and the text of each of our lives must
meet, but feminist women and men do not necessarily believe
that the text of the biblical witness takes precedence in that
meeting. Perhaps a more accurate way of speaking about this
meeting is that the biblical text and the text of women's lives
inform, broaden, and deepen the witness and power of each
other. This being true as a way of beginning to take our own
lives of faith more seriously, women weave themselves throughout their proclamations. Self-revelation is a distinctive point of
emphasis in feminist women's preaching.

Imagination. "Since the imagination allows us to 'see visions'
and 'dream dreams,' it is a pentecostal power, enabling Chris-
tians to move forward in history. . . . The imagination not only
shows us a possible future; it evokes the energies needed to
participate in the coming of that future."[9]
In some basic and fundamental way, Christian feminist
women know that the language, symbols, images, and rituals of
our faith have failed us. In the face of such truth, many are
experiencing immobilizing despair. I believe there are just as
many women, and many men, however, who have begun the
difficult and creative imaginative task of transforming every
strand of the language and symbol system of Christianity. Feminist women preachers within the Christian faith are playing a
significant role in this linguistic and symbolic reshaping of our
tradition.
As Kathleen Fischer expresses, "Images and symbols shape
experience on levels deeper than explanations. They survive in

the imagination, and it is there that they must be transformed."[10]

It is not accidental that women preachers often use rich imagery, poetic language, and imaginative stories in their preaching. If we ever are to arrive at new places of possibility, the imagination of the human family—individually and collectively—must be engaged. For feminist women preachers in the Christian church, the use of the imagination is not an artistic luxury but a vital necessity in our work as weavers of the word. The imagination not only allows us to envision a future where justice is pervasive and our own marginality ceases to exist, but it also gives us the creative and persistent energy and hope to bring that kind of future into being.

> Feminist theologians, aiming to create theologies shaped by female experiences previously unacknowledged and unattended to in Christian tradition, need quite different criteria for adequacy. . . . Imagination is as political as language is. Thus, images, rather than conceptual discourse or linear logic, are the roots of feminist theology, our primary language.[11]

Women use images to understand and claim their own life experiences, for naming those things that have never been named before in human history demands the language of imaginative possibility. My central focus on weaving as the organizing image of this entire work on feminist preaching is a powerful illustration. To express the distinctiveness of preaching from a feminist perspective through the use of an expansive, visionary image like weaving seems the only vital way to construct a picture of a new reality in our world and in our churches. Any other kind of language would have been inadequate.

Women place a strong emphasis on imagination and image out of both necessity and vision. It is our everyday naming of reality that literally brings women into being in a world where our invisibility and silence are still devastatingly real. It is also a language of hope, beckoning us to weave one more strand—and one more strand, and one more strand—into the tapestry of personal and social transformation.

Rhythm

Rhythm is a sense of continuity or recurrence, a succession
of spaced intervals. In a visual design rhythm causes the
eye to travel from one part of the composition to another
until the entire work has been perceived. . . . Rhythm helps
to create the particular atmosphere or expression of any
design.[12]

To ask what the rhythm of preaching from a feminist perspective might be is to ask the final integrative question. It is also
to ask the finely tuned artistic question, for this is not a question
of meaning or insight; rather this is a question of character,
spirit, or ambience. It is actually a question that should be
answered by the viewer, the hearer, those for whom the artistic
creation was intended. It is the community of faith who ultimately must give witness to the spirit of transformation reflected
in this preaching. That witness already surrounds us in the form
of increasing numbers of the Christian community who articulate with their voices and their lives the feminist vision of transformation.

Being a part of that Christian community, I believe feminist
preaching at its very finest should feel like an art piece and have
the spirit of transformation. An art piece invites us into its
reality, captures our imagination, and calls forth in us a touch
of emotion, a new awareness, an expanded vision. Transformation claims us, changes us forever, and leaves us with a new
identity. As women preachers in the Christian church weave
together expanded understandings of what it means to be
human, the critique and vision of feminism, and the good news
of faith, it is my hope that communities might feel compelled
to change as they are invited to new life.

Notes

Chapter 1. Weaving: Vision and Craft

1. Else Regensteiner, *The Art of Weaving* (New York: Van Nostrand Reinhold Co., 1981), p. 7.

2. Letter from James Cox, The Southern Baptist Theological Seminary, Louisville, Kentucky. Used by permission.

3. Letter from Raymond Bailey, The Southern Baptist Theological Seminary, Louisville, Kentucky. Used by permission.

4. Letter from Susan E. Davies, Bangor Theological Seminary, Bangor, Maine. Used by permission.

5. Conversation with Deane Kemper, Gordon-Conwell Theological Seminary, South Hamilton, Massachusetts. Used by permission.

6. Conversation with Bonnie Benda, Iliff School of Theology, Denver, Colorado. Used by permission.

7. Helen Gray Crotwell, ed., *Women and the Word—Sermons* (Philadelphia: Fortress Press, 1978).

8. *Spinning a Sacred Yarn: Women Speak from the Pulpit* (New York: Pilgrim Press, 1982).

9. Ella Pearson Mitchell, ed., *Those Preachin' Women: Sermons by Black Women Preachers* (Valley Forge, Pa.: Judson Press, 1985).

10. Charles D. Hackett, ed., *Women of the Word: Contemporary Sermons by Women Clergy* (Atlanta: Susan Hunter Publishing, 1985).

11. Ibid., p. 16.

12. Jean Wilson, *Weaving Is for Anyone* (New York: D. Van Nostrand Co., 1967), from the foreword.

13. Regensteiner, *The Art of Weaving,* p. 115.

14. Paula Gunn Allen, *The Sacred Hoop: Recovering the Feminine in American Indian Traditions* (Boston: Beacon Press, 1986). Allen

speaks throughout about Grandmother Spider, Spider Woman, and various other names for the same deity or supernatural being.

15. Mary E. Black, *Key to Weaving: A Textbook of Hand-Weaving Techniques and Pattern Drafts for the Beginning Weaver* (Milwaukee: Bruce Publishing Co., 1945), p. 9.

16. William Schulz, "Mirrors Never Lie? The Existential Dimension of Preaching," in William Schulz, ed., *Transforming Words* (Boston: Skinner House Books, 1984), pp. 44, 45.

17. Marjorie Agosin, "Needle and Thread Warriors: Women in Chile," *Woman of Power: Woman as Warrior,* no. 3 (Winter/Spring 1986), pp. 34, 35.

Chapter 2. Weaver: Woman as Preacher

1. Nell Znamierowski, *Step-by-Step Weaving* (New York: Golden Press, 1967), pp. 5, 7.

2. See John Killinger, *Fundamentals of Preaching* (Philadelphia: Fortress Press, 1985), p. 33.

3. Carol Tavris and Carole Wade, *The Longest War: Sex Differences in Perspective* (San Diego: Harcourt Brace Jovanovich, 1977), p. 78.

4. Ann Belford Ulanov, *Receiving Woman: Studies in the Psychology and Theology of the Feminine* (Philadelphia: Westminster Press, 1981), p. 116.

5. Carol Gilligan, *In a Different Voice: Psychological Theory and Women's Development* (Cambridge, Mass.: Harvard University Press, 1982), p. 62.

6. Nancy Chodorow, *The Reproduction of Mothering: The Psychoanalysis and the Sociology of Gender* (Berkeley, Calif.: University of California Press, 1978), p. 169.

7. Jean Baker Miller, *Toward a New Psychology of Women* (Boston: Beacon Press, 1976), p. 83.

8. Luise Eichenbaum and Susie Orbach, *Understanding Women: A Feminist Psychoanalytic Approach* (New York: Basic Books, 1983), p. 45.

9. Miller, *Toward a New Psychology of Women,* p. 1.

10. Ibid., pp. 8, 29, 86.

11. Ibid., pp. 31–32, 38.

12. Ibid., p. 41.

13. Ibid., pp. 83, 86.

14. Ibid., p. 78.

15. Chodorow, *The Reproduction of Mothering,* p. 173.

16. Ibid., p. 47.

17. Ibid., p. 93.

18. Ibid., pp. 104–108.

19. Ibid., pp. 166–170.

20. Gilligan, *In a Different Voice,* pp. 1–2.

21. Ibid., p. 1.

22. Ibid., pp. 24–25.

23. Ibid., p. 49.

24. Ibid., p. 160.

25. Eichenbaum and Orbach, *Understanding Women,* pp. 7–8.

26. Ibid., p. 56.

27. Ibid., p. 176.

28. Julia Esquivel, *Threatened with Resurrection: Prayers and Poems from an Exiled Guatemalan* (Elgin, Ill.: Brethren Press, 1982), pp. 107–109.

Chapter 3. The Loom of Authority: Mutuality and Solidarity

1. Jane Redman, *Frame-Loom Weaving* (New York: Van Nostrand Reinhold Co., 1976), pp. 8, 9.

2. Barbara Brown Zikmund, "Feminist Consciousness in Historical Perspective," in Letty M. Russell, ed., *Feminist Interpretation of the Bible* (Philadelphia: Westminster Press, 1985), p. 21.

3. Letty M. Russell, "Authority and the Challenge of Feminist Interpretation," in Russell, ed., *Feminist Interpretation of the Bible,* p. 143.

4. I raise this question as a white, middle-class, Christian, Protestant woman, ordained in the United Methodist Church and having served the whole of my pastoral ministry in white, middle-class, suburban United Methodist churches. I am aware of the limitations of what I articulate, yet I feel this question to be basic to a new naming of authority.

5. James W. Cox, *Preaching: A Comprehensive Approach to the Design and Delivery of Sermons* (San Francisco: Harper & Row, 1985), pp. 19–22.

6. Fred B. Craddock, *Preaching* (Nashville: Abingdon Press, 1985), p. 24.

7. Letty M. Russell, *Household of Freedom: Authority in Feminist Theology* (Philadelphia: Westminster Press, 1987), pp. 34–35.

8. Suzanne Juhasz, *Naked and Fiery Forms: Modern American Poetry by Women, A New Tradition* (New York: Harper & Row, 1976), p. 205, quoted by Dorothy Smith in Julia A. Sherman and Evelyn Torton Beck, eds., *The Prism of Sex* (Madison, Wis.: University of Wisconsin Press, 1979), p. 146.

9. Ibid., p. 144.

10. Jean Baker Miller, *Toward a New Psychology of Women* (Boston: Beacon Press, 1976), p. 39.

11. Isabel Carter Heyward, *The Redemption of God: A Theology of Mutual Relation* (Washington, D.C.: University Press of America, 1982), pp. 41, 43.

12. Miller, *Toward a New Psychology of Women,* p. 116.

13. Ann Belford Ulanov, *Receiving Woman: Studies in the Psychology and Theology of the Feminine* (Philadelphia: Westminster Press, 1981), pp. 22, 23.

14. Ibid., pp. 131–147.

15. Miller, *Toward a New Psychology of Women,* p. 113.

16. Maria C. Lugones and Elizabeth V. Spelman, "Have We Got a Theory for You! Feminist Theory, Cultural Imperialism, and the Demand for 'The Woman's Voice,' " in Marilyn Pearsall, ed., *Women and Values: Readings in Recent Feminist Philosophy* (Belmont, Calif.: Wadsworth Publishing Co., 1986), p. 20.

17. Anne Cameron, *Daughters of Copper Woman* (Vancouver, B.C.: Press Gang Publishers, 1981), p. 53.

18. John Killinger, *Fundamentals of Preaching* (Philadelphia: Fortress Press, 1985), p. 4.

19. Nelle Morton, *The Journey Is Home* (Boston: Beacon Press, 1985), p. 181.

20. Elisabeth Schüssler Fiorenza, "From Study to Proclamation," in John Burke, ed., *A New Look at Preaching* (Wilmington, Del.: Michael Glazier, 1983), p. 48.

21. Killinger, *Fundamentals of Preaching,* p. 49.

22. Fred B. Craddock, *Overhearing the Gospel* (Nashville: Abingdon Press, 1978), p. 125.

23. Alice Walker, *Horses Make the Landscape Look More Beautiful* (San Diego: Harcourt Brace Jovanovich, 1984), p. 12.

Chapter 4. The Warp of Critique: New Theological Naming

1. Osma Gallinger Tod, *The Joy of Handweaving* (New York: Dover Publications, 1964), p. 71.

2. Beverly Wildung Harrison, "The Power of Anger in the Work of Love," in Carol Robb, ed., *Making the Connections: Essays in Feminist Social Ethics* (Boston: Beacon Press, 1985), p. 227.

3. Elisabeth Schüssler Fiorenza, *Bread Not Stone: The Challenge of Feminist Biblical Interpretation* (Boston: Beacon Press, 1984), p. 3.

4. Miska Miles, *Annie and the Old One* (Boston: Little, Brown & Co., 1971), p. 41.

5. Harrison in Robb, *Making the Connections,* p. 5.

6. Justo L. Gonzalez and Catherine G. Gonzalez, *Liberation Preaching: The Pulpit and the Oppressed* (Nashville: Abingdon Press, 1980), p. 16.

7. Richard Lischer, *A Theology of Preaching* (Nashville: Abingdon Press, 1981), pp. 27, 29.

8. Mary Daly, *Beyond God the Father: Toward a Philosophy of Women's Liberation* (Boston: Beacon Press, 1973), pp. 30, 31.

9. Ibid., pp. 40, 8.

10. Virginia Ramey Mollenkott, *The Divine Feminine: The Biblical Imagery of God as Female* (New York: Crossroad, 1983).

11. Isabel Carter Heyward, "An Unfinished Symphony of Liberation: The Radicalization of Christian Feminism Among White U.S. Women," *Journal of Feminist Studies in Religion,* vol. 1, no. 1 (Spring 1985), p. 108.

12. Rosemary Radford Ruether, *Sexism and God-Talk: Toward a Feminist Theology* (Boston: Beacon Press, 1983), pp. 61–63.

13. Ibid., pp. 64–66.

14. Ibid., pp. 65–66.

15. Ibid., p. 68.

16. Ibid., p. 69.

17. Ibid., p. 53.

18. Carol Christ, "Feminist Liberation Theology and Yahweh as Holy Warrior: An Analysis of Symbol," in Janet Kalen and Mary I. Buckley, eds., *Women's Spirit Bonding* (New York: Pilgrim Press, 1984), pp. 203–204.

19. Ibid., p. 207.

20. Ruether, *Sexism and God-Talk,* p. 61.

21. Mud Flower Collective, *God's Fierce Whimsy: Christian Feminism and Theological Education* (New York: Pilgrim Press, 1985), p. 158.

22. Sallie McFague, *Metaphorical Theology: Models of God in Religious Language* (Philadelphia: Fortress Press, 1982), p. 193.

23. Ibid., p. 146.

24. Sallie McFague, *Models of God: Theology for an Ecological Nuclear Age* (Philadelphia: Fortress Press, 1987), pp. 91–174.

25. Ibid., p. 60.

26. Robert W. Duke, *The Sermon as God's Word: Theologies for Preaching* (Nashville: Abingdon Press, 1980), p. 13.

27. Patricia Wilson-Kastner, *Faith, Feminism, and the Christ* (Philadelphia: Fortress Press, 1983), p. 4.

28. Isabel Carter Heyward, *The Redemption of God: A Theology of Mutual Relation* (Washington, D.C.: University Press of America, 1982), p. 34.

29. Ibid., pp. 38, 39, 40.

30. Ibid., pp. 44–59.

31. Harrison in Robb, *Making the Connections,* pp. 18, 19.

32. Ibid., p. 19.

33. McFague, *Metaphorical Theology,* pp. 48–52.

34. Rita Nakashima Brock, "The Feminist Redemption of Christ," in Judith Wiedman, ed., *Christian Feminism* (San Francisco: Harper & Row, 1984), pp. 57, 63, 69, 74.

35. Mervyn A. Warren, *Black Preaching: Truth and Soul* (Washington, D.C.: University Press of America, 1977), p. 12.

36. Katie Geneva Cannon, "The Emergence of Black Feminist Consciousness," in Letty M. Russell, ed., *Feminist Interpretation of the Bible* (Philadelphia: Westminster Press, 1985), p. 40.

37. Ella Pearson Mitchell, ed., *Those Preachin' Women: Sermons by Black Women Preachers* (Valley Forge, Pa.: Judson Press, 1985).

38. McFague, *Metaphorical Theology,* p. 51.

39. Isabel Carter Heyward, quotes Sölle in *Our Passion for Justice: Images of Power, Sexuality, and Liberation* (New York: Pilgrim Press, 1984), p. 162.

40. Ibid., p. 216.

41. Elisabeth Schüssler Fiorenza, "The Will to Choose or to Reject: Continuing Our Critical Work," in Russell, ed., *Feminist Interpretation of the Bible,* p. 130.

42. William D. Thompson, *Preaching Biblically: Exegesis and Interpretation* (Nashville: Abingdon Press, 1981), pp. 40–43.

43. Fiorenza, *Bread Not Stone,* p. 18.

44. Ibid., p. 1.

45. Ibid., pp. 13, xiv.

46. Ibid., p. 15.

47. Duke, *The Sermon as God's Word,* p. 18.

48. Phyllis Trible, *God and the Rhetoric of Sexuality* (Philadelphia: Fortress Press, 1978), p. 8.

49. Fiorenza, *Bread Not Stone,* p. 18.

50. Letty M. Russell, ed., *Feminist Interpretation of the Bible* (Philadelphia: Westminster Press, 1985), p. 16.

51. Gonzalez and Gonzalez, *Liberation Preaching,* p. 40.

52. Fiorenza, *Bread Not Stone,* p. 19.

53. Trible, *God and the Rhetoric of Sexuality,* p. 202.

54. Phyllis Trible, *Texts of Terror* (Philadelphia: Fortress Press, 1984), p. 2.

55. Susan Beehler, "Steppin' Out," a song about celebrating the women who have gone on before us; the last verse is by Linda Coveleskie.

56. Fiorenza, *Bread Not Stone,* p. 20.

57. Ibid., pp. 20, 21.

58. Renita J. Weems, *Just a Sister Away: A Womanist Vision of Women's Relationships in the Bible* (San Diego: LuraMedia, 1988), p. ix.

59. Robert D. Young, *Religious Imagination: God's Gift to Prophets and Preachers* (Philadelphia: Westminster Press, 1979), pp. 30–37.

60. Henry F. May, *Protestant Churches and Industrial America* (New York: Harper & Brothers, 1949), pp. 216–224.

61. Judith L. Hoehler, "The Preacher as Prophet: The Relationship of Preaching to the Corporate Dimension," in William Schulz, ed., *Transforming Words: Six Essays on Preaching* (Boston: Skinner House Books, 1984), pp. 69, 85, 77.

Chapter 5. The Weft of Vision: Threads of Global Feminism

1. Osma Gallinger Tod, *The Joy of Handweaving* (New York: Dover Publications, 1964), pp. 110, 111.

2. Nan Benally, "Rug of Woven Magic," in Beth Brant, ed., *A Gathering of Spirit: Writing and Art by North American Indian Women* (Amherst, Mass.: Sinister Wisdom Books, 1984), pp. 182–183.

3. Jean Wilson, *Weaving Is for Anyone* (New York: D. Van Nostrand Co., 1967), p. 14.

4. Four books reveal this critique: Fred B. Craddock, *As One Without Authority* (Nashville: Abingdon Press, 1979), pp. 4–11; Willard F. Jabusch, *The Person in the Pulpit* (Nashville: Abingdon Press, 1980), pp. 114–116; William Schulz, ed., *Transforming Words: Six Essays on Preaching* (Boston: Skinner House Books, 1984), pp. x, xv; and Leander Keck, *The Bible in the Pulpit: The Renewal of Biblical Preaching* (Nashville: Abingdon Press, 1978), pp. 1, 41.

5. Elisabeth Schüssler Fiorenza, "From Study to Proclamation," in John Burke, ed., *A New Look at Preaching* (Wilmington, Del.: Michael Glazier, 1983), p. 45.

6. Carol Christ, *Diving Deep and Surfacing: Women Writers on Spiritual Quest* (Boston: Beacon Press, 1980), p. 24.

7. Annie Cheatham and Mary Clare Powell, *This Way Daybreak*

Comes: Women's Values and the Future (Philadelphia: New Society Publishers, 1986), pp. xix, xxi.

8. Ibid., p. xxi.

9. Bonnie Thornton-Dill, "Interview on Envisioning a Feminist World," *Woman of Power: Envisioning a Feminist World,* no. 2 (Summer 1985), p. 33.

10. Adele Smith-Penniman, ibid., p. 31.

11. Char McKee, "Feminism: A Vision of Love," *Woman of Power: Envisioning a Feminist World,* no. 2 (Summer 1985), p. 5.

12. Delores S. Williams, "Women's Oppression and Lifeline Politics in Black Women's Religious Narratives," *Journal of Feminist Studies in Religion,* vol. 1, no. 1 (Spring 1985), pp. 70, 71.

13. Barbara Smith, ed., *Home Girls: A Black Feminist Anthology* (New York: Kitchen Table: Women of Color Press, 1983), p. xxxix.

14. Ibid., p. xxix.

15. Audre Lorde, *Chosen Poems—Old and New* (New York: W. W. Norton & Co., 1982), pp. 49–50.

16. Cherrie Moraga and Gloria Anzaldua, eds., *This Bridge Called My Back: Writings by Radical Women of Color* (New York: Kitchen Table: Women of Color Press, 1981).

17. Isabel Carter Heyward, *Our Passion for Justice: Images of Power, Sexuality, and Liberation* (New York: Pilgrim Press, 1984).

18. Beverly Wildung Harrison, in Carol Robb, ed., *Making the Connections: Essays in Feminist Social Ethics* (Boston: Beacon Press, 1985), pp. 244, 240.

19. Heyward, *Our Passion for Justice,* preface.

20. Ibid., pp. 184, 212.

21. Harrison in Robb, *Making the Connections,* pp. 155, 166.

22. Yvonne Duffy, . . . *All Things Are Possible* (Ann Arbor, Mich.: A. J. Garvin & Associates, 1981), p. 12.

23. Susan E. Browne, Debra Connors, and Nanci Stern, eds., *With the Power of Each Breath: A Disabled Women's Anthology* (Pittsburgh and San Francisco: Cleis Press, A Women's Publishing Company, 1985), pp. 13, 14.

24. Kathy Black, a United Methodist clergywoman from the Baltimore Annual Conference. This quotation comes from a conversation with Kathy about her commitment to the deaf community.

25. Judy Small, "Speaking Hands and Hearing Eyes," from an album entitled *Mothers, Daughters, Wives* (Redwood Records, 1984, Oakland, Calif.).

26. Sharon D. Welch, *Communities of Resistance and Solidarity: A*

Feminist Theology of Liberation (Maryknoll, N.Y.: Orbis Books, 1985), pp. 72, 80.

27. John Killinger, *Fundamentals of Preaching* (Philadelphia: Fortress Press, 1985), pp. 10, 28.

28. Fred B. Craddock, *Overhearing the Gospel* (Nashville: Abingdon Press, 1978), pp. 23–25.

29. Jan Powers Miller, "Makin' Room for the Silences." This song was created in response to a "fishbowl experience" at the Northeast United Methodist Clergywomen's Conference, May 1986, where the group attempted to hear the "silenced voices in our midst."

30. Gwyn Kirk, "Our Greenham Common: Not Just a Place but a Movement," p. 80, a draft of a future article. Gwyn is a friend and a peace activist from England traveling in the United States attempting to educate people about the situation at Greenham Common, 1985.

31. Ibid., p. 81.

32. Ibid., pp. 83, 85.

33. Holly Near, "The Great Peace March," from an album entitled *Singing with You* (Redwood Records, 1986, Oakland, Calif.).

34. Heyward, *Our Passion for Justice,* p. 79.

35. Harrison in Robb, *Making the Connections,* p. 175.

36. Dorothee Sölle, *Choosing Life* (Philadelphia: Fortress Press, 1981), p. 16.

37. Dorothee Sölle, *Of War and Love* (Maryknoll, N.Y.: Orbis Books, 1983), pp. 32, 33.

38. Pam McAllister, ed., *Reweaving the Web of Life: Feminism and Nonviolence* (Philadelphia: New Society Publishers, 1982), p. 28.

39. Harrison in Robb, *Making the Connections,* p. 19.

40. Welch, *Communities,* p. 51.

41. Ibid., pp. 7, 4.

42. Heyward, *Our Passion for Justice,* pp. 171, 172.

43. Harrison in Robb, *Making the Connections,* p. 12.

44. Sweet Honey in the Rock is a Black woman's music group: visionary, confrontive, powerful. They seek to make connections between all issues that influence women's lives.

45. Holly Near is a white woman who has been singing in the women's community for many years. She produces music that weaves together diverse and complex issues of justice for women and for our world.

46. Judy Chicago is a woman artist who is best known for her outstanding historical art piece *The Dinner Party* and her work celebrating the joy, pain, and experience of women giving birth to human

life, *The Birth Project.* Both pieces of work have been collaborative art expressions, involving large numbers of women in their creation. Each piece of work has been a powerful celebration of the concrete experiences of being a woman.

47. Donna Kate Rushin's "The Bridge Poem," in *This Bridge Called My Back: Writings by Radical Women of Color* (see note 16), has become a very important poem in my life, helping me understand more fully the way women must always be the "bridge" to other people's understanding of their experience and their sense of self.

48. Adrienne Rich's *The Dream of a Common Language: Poems 1974–1977* (New York: W. W. Norton & Co., 1978) is a book of poetry about women's experience. Rich's "drive to connect" is what motivates the use of the words "dream of a common language."

Chapter 6. Weave Variations: Principles of Design

1. Shirley E. Held, *Weaving: A Handbook for Fiber Craftsmen* (New York: Holt, Rinehart & Winston, 1973), p. 301.

2. Ibid., pp. 309, 310.

3. Ibid., p. 310.

4. Ibid.

5. Carol Christ, *Diving Deep and Surfacing: Women Writers on Spiritual Quest* (Boston: Beacon Press, 1980), pp. 23, 24.

6. Held, *Weaving,* pp. 311, 312.

7. Ibid., p. 313.

8. Mud Flower Collective, *God's Fierce Whimsy: Christian Feminism and Theological Education* (New York: Pilgrim Press, 1985), p. 156.

9. Kathleen R. Fischer, *The Inner Rainbow: The Imagination in Christian Life* (New York: Paulist Press, 1983), p. 24.

10. Ibid., p. 111.

11. Mud Flower Collective, *God's Fierce Whimsy,* pp. 157, 158.

12. Held, *Weaving,* p. 314.

Index